Reviews of *Imaginations to Revelations*

God still performs wonders and He still changes lives. That is the story of *Imaginations to Revelations*. This is the account of a living miracle. From alcohol and drugs to a life of sexual addiction and promiscuity, Lisa's story casts the spotlight of God's grace on the darkest corners of life. Her story is compelling, raw, and redemptive. If you are on a quest for hope and freedom, *Imaginations to Revelations* may be the most important book you read all year!

Dr. Mark Denison
Founder, There's Still Hope

Lisa's life is nothing short of a miracle. Her transparency and the steps to freedom she shares in *Imaginations to Revelations* will give anyone reading Lisa's book hope and encouragement.

Stan Pavkovich
Pastor, Church of the Cross

Imaginations to Revelations

Lisa Marie Ringland

Imaginations to Revelations

Lisa Marie Ringland

Published by Austin Brothers Publishing,
Fort Worth, Texas
www.abpbooks.com

ISBN 978-0-9891027-9-7
Library of Congress Control Number:2019919175
Copyright © 2019 by Lisa Marie Ringland

ALL RIGHTS RESERVED. *No part of this book may be reproduced in any form without permission in writing from the publisher, except in the case of brief quotations embodied in critical reviews or articles.*

Printed in the United States of America
2019 -- First Edition

This book is dedicated to

My Lord and Savior Jesus Christ,

My loving parents, Donald and Mary Ringland, for countless prayers and perseverance through my addiction and rebellion

Sheila Donoghue, my sponsor, who guided me through the 12 steps to freedom

Judy Willis, who counseled and instructed me in the early stages of spiritual warfare and biblical truth.

I am indebted and ever grateful to God for his rescuing, redeeming love and power, and all those who had an instrumental part in my faith and journey.

Kimberly for being a faithful friend who gave me a chance when no one else would

Almighty God, hear my prayer. Remove scales from eyes. Open ears and soften hearts to be prepared to receive your word. Let any reader who suffers from addiction, worthlessness, emptiness, or rejection, find purpose, meaning, and significance in you. Let the raw honesty of my struggles comfort those in need of hope. Provide a way out and transformation that points the way to you. Thank you for touching lives with this book and bringing people out of darkness, drawing them into your presence and light amen.

Contents

Hitting Bottom	1
Transparency Versus Secrecy	7
No Faith, Too Little Faith, Unemployment	17
Miracles from God	25
God's Interruption and Intervention	31
Big Faith	39
Building a Life	61
Breaking Financial Strongholds	75
Dating Danny	87
Humiliations Before Humility	97
Closing Doors	113
Opening the Door For the Enemy	125
Waiting on God	131
Growing Up: Mature Faith	145

Introduction

Hitting Bottom

My entire life I have struggled to gain acceptance; feeling inferior, disconnected, and set apart without comprehending why. I was different from my parents and peers, especially in the area of male attraction and my sexuality.

Although this is not a biography of my entire life, there is an important detail for understanding this part of my journey. I was adopted as an infant. I don't bring up this fact to accuse my adoptive parents in any way or suggest that I was raised in some dysfunctional situation. I was the consequence of teen pregnancy and probably the recipient of a genetic disposition toward alcoholism.

My mom and dad are strong Christians, and I was raised in a loving, Christian home. I am grateful for my upbringing. However, from an early age, it was evident that I had an unusual, abnormal, sexual curiosity. My father caught me experimenting as a child with my sexuality. I had an excessive and obsessive sex drive as a seven-year-old child. Clearly, I was a sex and love addict without even realizing and comprehending what it meant.

The Breaking of Me Was the Remaking of Me

"Boy crazy," as my mom would say, was an understatement. In kindergarten, I would tackle the boys and kiss them if they were caught. By age 12, because I was seeking acceptance from the crowd I was with, I turned to alcohol and drugs, but sex, love, acceptance, and approval-seeking truly were my primary strongholds. Initially, using drugs and alcohol was social, experimental, and fun, but it is progressive and fatal when prolonged and continued. I was sinking into darkness, and oblivious that there was anything wrong.

There have been studies about adopted children having abandonment issues. Understanding this part of my background explains much of the stronghold's emotional, mental, and sexual grip it had on my life.

Obtaining factual information about the psyche of the brain later on as an adult helped me understand there is a part of the brain that knows the child has been displaced from its mother. Also, after much research during my recovery, I've come to understand about generational curses as well as a genetic disposition. Enduring decades of trouble, failed relationships, abusive drugs, and drinking, I've had countless humiliations, failures, and bottoms. Despite everything, I had never been all-in recovery. Physically abstinent, yet never dealing with trauma, co-dependency or psychological issues.

Until now, I had never fully surrendered. Like every addict, I had many attempts at getting sober and cleaning up my life, but I never fully surrendered to Christ. However, I arrived at the point where I felt like I was running out of options and time. Beaten down once again, I made another attempt to get clean.

The reason I'm writing this book is because God has called me to speak about the darkness in which I once lived, and His miraculous orchestration of events and unexplainable circumstances that only point to His rescuing, redemptive, amazing power.

Many in my condition don't get out. One of the things you will learn about in this book is my gratitude. I could have been another depressing statistic, yet through God's amazing grace, relentless love, and intentional pursuit, the exact opposite is true.

Going to 12-step meetings was merely a beginning that I had attempted before with little or no resolve, so I was quite unsure of myself that I would even succeed this time. After all, my track record wasn't the greatest. What would be the difference from my last attempt? In the past, after obtaining physical sobriety, it was only a matter of time until I caved and gave up.

I was physically sober for a few years each time, but my desire for sex and men would always be the primary distraction of my focus. This always led inevitably to my demise. Being blocked unconsciously from God's power, I began a slow regression into worldliness, codependency, and ultimately addiction all over again. This cycle was predictable and reoccurring.

Looking back, I realize that I stayed out there for a good ten years, a decade, wishing and wanting to get sober, but I never knew how much destruction I brought upon myself and how much reconstruction was necessary to rebuild my life. Knowing full well how much hard work lay ahead for me to overcome legal, social, employment, and financial devastation—I didn't have it in me. So, I put it off as long as possible. I knew the struggle, the humiliation of coming back in and starting over. I knew the difficulty of being real, honest, and raw. The requirement to be willing, disciplined, and taking the hard way rather than shortcuts was just too much for me to endure, so I put it off as long as possible.

Sustaining my lifestyle while doing drugs was made possible only because of my involvement in the sex industry. The thought of minimum wage and an average, menial job, taking a bus or bicycle was unthinkable. It was beneath me, so I stayed out there for a long time and continued using and living in darkness.

Chapter 1

Transparency Versus Secrecy

Starting over this time, I was afraid, uncertain of how to function. I knew I needed help and still concerned about defeat. My decline brought me to the point of sharing an apartment with my female roommate who was my using partner as well as my pimp. By this time, all who used with me were fed up with my progression and decline. How sad when the people using right along with you are strongly suggesting that you should stop and need to get clean. I had already been arrested a couple of times, losing my vehicle and driver's license. I was bicycling or cabbing to meetings, arriving late, leaving early, not wanting anyone to get to know me. Doing the bare minimum by simply attending, staying on the edges of the fellowship, I remained full of fear and separation.

Being so unsure of myself, not wanting to get to know anyone or ever allow them to get to know me, I never spoke or engaged anyone face-to-face. In the middle of a crowded meeting, I was isolated and withdrawn. I took notice of a woman who was attending. I discovered later that she was living in the same apartment complex as me. My roommate mentioned I should ask this woman to sponsor me, and I reluctantly declined. Never would I approach or ask anyone! After all, they might reject or judge me once they got to know me. Having a sponsor would mean transparency about my lifestyle as a prostitute and this I could not allow.

The following progression is how I understood the process. You can understand why I hesitated to get started because I knew what was eventually required:

Engagement = Involvement
Involvement = Relationship
Relationship = Accountability
Accountability = Transparency
Accountability = Partnership
Transparency = Honesty
Partnership = Commitment
Commitment = Sacrifice

I was terrified of transparency because it meant honesty and disclosure of my sexual practices and deepest secrets. I feared that if you got to know me, you would disapprove, which meant you would reject and discard me. To be transparent was unveiling my deepest wound of abandonment, rejection, and unworthiness.

Eventually, I began to engage with this woman at groups with small talk. I would see her at the apartment pool and say hello. She offered rides, and once I trusted her, we began to develop a relationship. I finally took a risk and let her in on the reality of my lifestyle. For the first time, I worked through the process of uncovering every fear, shameful act, harm, and resentment.

This was the first time I ever involved another person in discovering and identifying my faults, discarding them one by one. I withheld nothing and became completely transparent and authentic. I honestly wanted to break chains and discard the bondage to begin my journey into freedom.

I went through every detail of my life, even talking with family, employers, and all the relationships where I caused harm. I was willing to rectify my actions and ask for forgiveness. It was the beginning of humility and willingness to do the things I've never done before.

At last, the desire to abstain from alcohol and narcotics overcame me. Never before did I have any power to deny my impulses and cravings. I was no longer delusional about consequences or the reality of what always precedes the first drink or drug. I was willing to bear the unbearable emotions of emptiness, loneliness, boredom, restlessness, and discontentment.

I understood that if I bear this condition temporarily, I won't regret the decision the following morning. If I partake in a temporary fix or momentary escape from my emotions or condition, my reality will return with even worse consequences – guilt, remorse, shame, along with compounded failure and hopelessness that were sure to follow. For the first time in a long time, I was staying sober and actually liberated by it. I was not just enduring the struggle; I sincerely wanted to live clean and free more than anything else.

> *Two people are better off than one, for they can help each other succeed. If one person falls, the other can reach out and help. But someone who falls alone is in real trouble. Likewise, two people lying close together can keep each other warm. But*

> *how can one be warm alone? A person standing alone can be attacked and defeated, but two can stand back-to-back and conquer. Three are even better, for a triple-braided cord is not easily broken. (Ecclesiastes 4:9-12)*

Paramount in my recovery today is being willing to accept advice and correction from a trusted friend. This person is my sponsor, whom I have permitted to know all there is to know about me as well as speak truthfully into my life. This provides an unbiased perspective. Especially if it is someone who has undergone similar temptations and struggles but experiences victory through God's word and power. Also, it promotes humility. The correct view of ourselves and our inadequacies is that we need reliance on others who are like-minded about God. Left alone, I have a distorted view of my own "skewed" perceptions, and a tendency to become proud, self-reliant, self-sufficient, and live by self-propulsion.

> *Whoever conceals their sins does not prosper, but the one who confesses and renounces them finds mercy. Blessed is the one who always trembles before God, but whoever hardens their heart falls into trouble. (Proverbs 28:13-14)*

Geographical Cures and Sole Ties

So many things had already been happening serendipitously. Was it happenstance or the powerful hand of God protecting me, rescuing me, pursuing me long before I ever chose him and his righteousness? I had been arrested for the second time for prostitution and given a sentence of 60 days in jail. I was infatuated with my boyfriend in addiction and looking forward to getting back together with him as soon as I got out.

However, my boyfriend was arrested on the day of my release from jail. He was snatched up and extradited from Florida to Oregon. He was labeled a habitual criminal in two different states and both states were in collaboration to get this man off the street and for him to serve time for his crimes. A coincidence or fate? From my perspective, it was purely divine intervention. God removed him from my life. Yet I had other plans. Plans to start fresh, start over, no ties or temptations from my friends or experiences in Florida. I would travel to Oregon to be with him as soon as he was released. We would begin our life together with a clean slate in another state. I was sure he wanted what I did. I was confident we were on the same page.

> *There is a way that appears to be right, but in the end it leads to death. (Proverbs 14:12)*

I moved across the country with my belongings and my two cats. The only thing that was right was my commitment to recovery. As soon as I arrived in Oregon, I called for help and became deeply involved in recovery groups and on a mission to find legitimate employment. This was my heart's desire, my longing for God, my commitment to regain and reconstruct a new life. I realize now how God had begun a new desire in me to move away from the old environment to make a fresh start somewhere new. I wanted to regain stability with him at the center of my life. I arrived in Oregon and got settled into a place with a friend before Frankie's release, which allowed me to become adapted and involved in a 12-Step community immediately. This was paramount for my successful recovery long term.

I was beginning to understand my inability to function without help, the need for community guidance and support. Something had already transpired within me. I can see now how God had orchestrated by design my boyfriend's arrest and my release. His extradition across the country prompted me to move there to remove myself from my roommate "Jezebel" and break free from the grip from that lifestyle. There were so many lessons to come, but this was the beginning of my journey into courage, commitment, and faith. With God's power, I moved from fear to faith and how to let go absolutely. Within the next few months, things would begin to be eradicated forever.

My Ex's Release from Prison

Within hours of my ex-boyfriend's release from prison, he was talking to me about acquiring medication and selling it. I knew that neither of us could hold anything without using it. I could not believe it. After everything I had been through, and the pull of this man and every man has had on me, I was actually defending the reality of both our addictions. He was using mild medication within days of his release.

For the first time in my life, I was determined to hold on to this new life I'd been given. I knew, without reservation, that a substance of any kind in any form in any way of using it would never work for me. I have finally conceded to my inner self that

I could never and would never be able to partake in a chemical in any form and be able to use moderately, safely, and stop abruptly. I have a complete inability for decision making after I have indulged. I understand the condition of having an allergy of the body and the complexity of this malady of my soul. This romantic delusion of us restarting a life together was crumbling all around me, shattering all my hopes and dreams.

Turning my focus to God, recovery, and support of those in the recovery community, I was becoming disenchanted with him by the day. It was spiraling into abandonment, neglect, disrespect, and isolation. After all I had envisioned about us was now turning out to be me and only me. His extradition forced our separation, allowing me to gain four months of clean time, and a foundation was laid.

There was already something profound about my conviction to abstain and stay connected. Sobriety was my utmost priority, so we remained living separately the entire time I was in Oregon. Our visits became more minimal, moving forward as my entire focus was staying sober as well as looking for legitimate employment. My full-time job became finding a job. I filled my life with constructive activities, which helped minimize any loneliness for my ex. Scales were being lifted from my eyes. What I wanted then was becoming less attractive and unappealing all the time.

Chapter 2

No Faith, Too Little Faith, Unemployment

Getting into the mainstream of society and the workforce was enlightening. It revealed my fear, self-doubt, and apprehension, along with my inabilities and inexperience. Going on job hunts and interviews absolutely terrified and paralyzed me. I was inexperienced, unqualified, and technically illiterate. With everything being done online made it impossible for me. I had nothing to put on a resume because I hadn't been legit in years. It was a nightmare!! Like an alien having a human experience, feeling foreign and fake. I didn't know what I was doing and petrified of being found out!

Three months of searching and unemployment went on, and I was becoming frustrated, desperate, and hopeless. Early on, I remember venting and complaining constantly. I wanted others to sympathize with my misfortune and plight in life; I remained a victim. Woe is me! I had it so rough, so hard!

Though failing to realize it, I had created these miserable circumstances for myself by a series of negligence, self-centeredness, and self-absorbed choices, living in a quick, fast, demonic lifestyle. Now that I had chosen to untangle this web and stop, it was like hitting the breaks, and everything sailed forward—disheveled, chaotic and a mess! Wide awake, I now realized how dysfunctional and abnormal my previous existence was. How many problems I actually had now, ready to deal with them rather than run from them.

Belief Versus Faith

Continual complaining regarding not attaining employment led a woman to boldly interject in front of a crowded room, "Where's your faith woman?"

I was appalled, offended, not to mention embarrassed, "What do you mean? I have faith! I believe!"

At that moment, her truth pierced my heart. It shook me to the core of my being. It alerted me to the fact that even though I believed in God, I had no faith whatsoever. Not in God, not in others, not even in myself. I had no faith in anyone but my parents and my sponsor. After all, my life was a continuous succession of mistrust, utilized to protect myself against dishonest addicts, thieves, and abusive men.

I had no trust that God was actually taking care of me in the present, and no faith whatsoever that he was going to do anything for me in the future. I had no faith at all. I realized I had come to faith only by salvation, and belief that he did exist. Jesus was the living God, the son of God resurrected, but otherwise, I had no faith in him whatsoever. I didn't rely on, depend on, trust in, confide in, expect from, hold fast to God at all.

I had grown up believing in God but realized now looking back, I had no concept or understanding in his power, his word, or his promises! None at all! I was used to self-propulsion and grabbing at everything I needed in life. Aggressively going after, driven, of course, to get whatever I needed whenever

I needed it. I needed to make it happen, or it wasn't going to happen and so I did.

I realized that God's testing, trials, and difficulties, along my earliest journey, was the mere beginning of his power and provision. I realize now that he will always take care of me because he always has, and I've been through so much. But then I had no clue that this was a revelation and awakening to me.

"What do you mean? I have faith!"

But what I really meant though, I have none at all. Knowing about God isn't living and abiding in his presence, trusting in him that the very hairs on my head are numbered, and he is sovereign with every detail concerning me. Simply believing that there is a God isn't living by faith at all.

After continued unemployment, I caved in. I called my ex-roommate to resume illegitimate earnings in prostitution. I couldn't take it anymore. The first miracle God provided was a phone call for a job. No exaggeration within one hour of that phone call to her, my first job offer came by literally calling me into work right over the phone. I canceled my plans with her, explaining I just got called in to my first real job and after his miraculous provision, I couldn't ignore his hand or go through with the illegitimate plan.

Finally, I went to work! God wasn't going to let me continue in that lifestyle of perversion any longer. He absolutely intervened; supernaturally intervened. The precision of his timing to this day is undeniably mind-blowing. I'm ever grateful for his protection, rescuing, redemption, even though I didn't fully understand his divine orchestration or his sovereign power at all. He was allowing me to be stretched by this trial of unemployment to enlarge my faith, and misunderstanding God as well as trials, I perceived it as a curse, a punishment and a lack of care for me.

Through faith we understand that the world was made by the Word of God. Things we see were made from what could not be seen. (Hebrews 11:3)

> *For you formed my inward parts; you knitted me together in my mother's womb. I praise you for I am fearfully and wonderfully made. Wonderful are your works my soul knows it well. My frame was not hidden from you when I was being made in secret intricately woven in the depths of the earth. Your eyes saw my unformed body; in your book were written every one of them the days were formed for me, when as yet there was none of them. (Psalm 139:13-16)*

A man cannot please God unless he has faith. Anyone who comes to God must believe that he exist. That one must also know that God gives what is promised to the one who keeps on looking for Him. (see Hebrews 11:6)

Looking back, I see I was hanging on, enduring it with my own strength, will, and understanding. I had no idea, down to the last detail, God had already ordained in his book all the days of my life before I was even born. My tiny seed of faith was about to be expanded by God through hardship and difficulty. It would be developed and expanded over testing and time. Faith not tested is weak. Faith under trial is purified by the crucible.

Fight or Flight Mentality

I was doing well in the mainstream of society and the workplace, but in personal relationships, I still had no coping skills, assertiveness, communication, or courage. This would be a problem that would take years to master.

My ex-boyfriend was so bad on heroin that I could not be around him. It disgusted and frustrated me. The roommate I was renting a room from, was asking for a lot of money for a phone bill that

I racked up being on her plan. She also asked me to split her deposit on the house, and I reminded her about the money I sent to her from Florida before I even moved to Oregon. This secured me a few months of rent. There was never enough money for her and never enough courage or confidence in me.

Every day I wondered what I should do, unsure of how to cope, confront, or manage. I just wanted to run, to get out and go back. Not to drugs, but I wanted to go home and run away. To do that, I needed to secure an apartment, plane ticket, moving expenses. The only solution I could fathom was returning to prostitution. Not permanently but a quick solution to run home with enough money for a new fresh start. I hate even to admit it to a world peering into my life now, knowing everything there is to know about me, but this above everything else had the strongest hold on my life. It just seemed the only way to resolve the matter and the only way to get ahead.

It never occurred to me to keep working, find another place to rent for a fresh start, and make minimum payments for the phone bill. Making an effort was better than nonpayment, right? Running was easier, and using my body was routine.

Relying on God's wisdom and power was incomprehensible. I didn't even know it was available, I didn't understand then it was a walk of faith, a discipline to seek God's guidance and wisdom, and asking for his help. Understanding and believing in the depths of my soul that God is who he says he is was difficult for me. I didn't understand that he cannot lie, and his character is unchanging. I had "belief" in him, but again, I had no clue that if I asked and stayed faithful to him, he would undeniably deliver me. Again, no faith at all! So, I quit… my job, my roommate, Oregon, also God, and myself.

Chapter 3

Miracles from God

I packed up my belongings, shipped them home to my parents, booked a plane ticket to New York, and reserved a hotel room. I went back to the only thing I thought I knew. I planned to return to Florida (home) via New York. The reason I wanted to go there was to earn money to make it possible for me to make it home to Florida and secure the travel for myself, my animals, my belongings, as well as securing rent and a security deposit for my own apartment. Prostitution was the quickest way I knew to make that amount of money.

Glouster

In preparation for the trip to New York, I was boarding the plane with my kitty cat Glouster in his carrier for the flight. Approaching the entrance of the cargo flight area, he escaped his carrier as it was not secured. The more I chased him, the deeper and further he ran. I was devastated, calling out to him, searching for most of the night!

Eventually, the police arrived and directed me to vacate the premises because I was endangering myself by walking on the shoulder and median of the road. Forced to surrender my search, I canceled my flight and decided to stay until I gave it all I had, knowing if I didn't find him, he would be lost forever.

For two days, I went to every cargo carrier, petitioning help for this lost cat that I deeply loved. Giving my contact information to each employee, weeping to them in hopes someone might encounter him in his instinctual need for food. The hotel concierge was my last contact and last hope. This man would be the very person who ultimately discovered my little lost Glouster at the exact place he had escaped.

Ironically, he just so happened to be driving two flight attendants to their car parked in front of the cargo carrier where Glouster had escaped. One of them heard a violent cry and asked: "Did you hear that?"

The concierge replied, "That's that lady's cat!"

Glouster came to the woman, but when he realized it was not me, he clawed her and jumped down, running away again.

The concierge frantically called me stating that he had seen my cat, explaining what had happened. He agreed to pick me up, bringing the carrier and wet food. I called for Glouster, heard him crying, and saw that he was severely spooked. He was frantically running and hiding in the shrubbery.

I knew the only way to capture him was to lure him with the wet food. Sitting Indian style like a statue calling out to him, allowing him to come closer, I cracked the can of wet food so he could hear it. Sitting with the can between my legs completely frozen, he crawled up to me. Allowing him to indulge in a few bites, I suddenly seized him by the nape of the neck, quickly harnessing him in my arms. I ran across the road where the concierge's vehicle was and securely placed him inside his carrier, now knowing he was safe with me. We headed back to the hotel room with him safe.

What makes this event even more spectacular is the fact he informed me in the car traveling back to the hotel, that he never goes or drives to this parking area. Due to the fact he encountered two flight attendants and all three of them were departing their jobs at the same time, these two women politely asked if he could drive them to their vehicles. They just happened to be in the cargo parking lot where Glouster had escaped and was, in fact, still lost and hiding.

The Parting of My Red Sea

This was the miraculous hand of God parting the Red Sea for me that would change my life forever. To this day, I weep with deep thankfulness and amazement to God for rescuing my little animal, my friend, my baby. Having no children, he is like my child. I'll never forget this supernatural act.

After this happened, especially the first few years, I would awaken with this miracle in the forefront of my memory full of praise and worship toward God. Filled with deep emotion and humility, I was reassured of God's power, presence, and miraculous hand touching my life. Family and friends were praying, my prayers and supplication rising to God "Please bring Glouster back to me. Please bring him home." Our prayers were heard and answered. God was moved with great compassion and acted on my behalf.

Imaginations to Revelations

After getting my animal safely back, I proceeded to New York. Despite this profound miracle, I was determined to follow through with my excursion, rationalizing, minimizing and justifying my conduct as an absolute urgency to obtain necessary revenue, I now had the last missing piece of the puzzle back in my arms to proceed. I was only holding and delaying all for the sake of rescuing Glouster. Now everything was in place to continue on my destination.

Chapter 4

God's Interruption and Intervention

Stern discipline awaits anyone who leaves the path; the one who hates correction will die. (Proverbs 15:10)

"Stolen water is sweet; food eaten in secret is delicious!" But little do they know that the dead are there, that her guests are deep in the realm of the dead. (Proverbs 9:17-18)

The note in my study Bible explains, "There's something hypnotic and intoxicating about wickedness. One sin leads to another. Don't be deceived; sin is dangerous. Before reaching for the forbidden fruit, take a long look at what happens to those who eat it. (Chronological Study Bible)

After arriving in New York, I worked for a few days before my mother called to tell me that my mother-in-law was searching for me and was adamant about contacting me. Then my mother asked, "Are you in New York?"

"How did you know?" I replied, covering my response with a lie.

When I finally did contact my mother-in-law, she told me that she knew I was in two states, California and New York. I was on the west coast but not California, "Oregon is close enough to California I would say."

But how did she know this? Mind you; I hadn't spoken to her or my husband in at least five years. Out of the clear blue, she was contacting me and vigorously pursuing me. When I told her I was in Oregon and now New York, she proceeded to enlighten me with a dream from God. He came to her in a dream and urgently warned her that someone was going to take advantage of me and hurt me.

I got scared. I knew my clock was ticking and running out of time. I also knew God was warning me, I have tested the Lord God long enough, living in rebellion and defiance. I know now I was stepping outside of God's umbrella of protection, and it was going to rain. Patiently, God had waited for me; lovingly, he had spared me from violence and death. Mercifully and graciously he would again and again take me back only for me to pull up, pull out, and spit in his face and defy him.

> *"Therefore, you prostitute, hear the word of the Lord! This is what the Sovereign Lord says: Because you poured out your lust and exposed your naked body in your promiscuity with your lovers, and because of all your detestable idols, and because you gave them your children's blood, therefore I am going to gather all your lovers, with whom you found pleasure, those you loved as well as those you hated. I will gather them against you from all around and will strip you in front of them, and they will see you stark naked. I will sentence you to the punishment of women who commit adultery and who shed blood; I will bring on you the blood vengeance of my wrath and jealous anger. Then I will deliver you into the hands of your lovers, and they will tear down your mounds and destroy your lofty shrines. They will strip you of your clothes and take your fine jewelry and leave you stark naked. They will bring a mob against you, who will stone you and hack you to pieces with their swords.*

They will burn down your houses and inflict punishment on you in the sight of many women. I will put a stop to your prostitution, and you will no longer pay your lovers. Then my wrath against you will subside and my jealous anger will turn away from you; I will be calm and no longer angry.

"Because you did not remember the days of your youth but enraged me with all these things, I will surely bring down on your head what you have done, declares the Sovereign Lord. Did you not add lewdness to all your other detestable practices? (Ezekiel 16:35-42)

His warning was strong, sincere, and final. This was going to be it. Within the same few days, my sponsor also called to see why I wasn't checking in with her. I casually admitted where I was. She drew a line in the sand; enough was enough! She fired me.

"After all this time, all the work we have done through the steps, what makes you think you can just take off, do your own thing, and wind up in some hotel room? You're on step to insanity; you're fired!"

She was also at a breaking point with me. Absolutely disgusted and finished with this unspiritual practice she could no longer condone, I was fired!!

At that moment, I was stunned, pierced with great fear, shock, and grief. This woman, this relationship, meant more to me than anything I've ever had before. I had never invested so much, revealed so much and took such a great risk with anyone ever before in my life. I've never been more earnest about recovery, more willing, honest and humble ever before in my history. Therefore, losing her was sealing my darkest fate.

I frantically begged her to give me another chance. Promising right then and there to stop and surrender. I made a decision right then. I wasn't willing to lose God, lose her, my soul, or my life. I called my pimp, quit, and booked a flight to return home.

The reason it is considered worse to God is because we know better. I knew better but proceeded against my inner consciousness and minimized my sin.

> *"This is what the Sovereign Lord says: I will deal with you as you deserve because you have despised my oath by breaking the covenant. Yet I will remember the covenant I made with you in the days of your youth, and I will establish an everlasting covenant with you. Then you will remember your ways and be ashamed when you receive your sisters, both those who are older than you and those who*

> *are younger. I will give them to you as daughters, but not on the basis of my covenant with you. So I will establish my covenant with you, and you will know that I am the Lord. Then, when I make atonement for you for all you have done, you will remember and be ashamed and never again open your mouth because of your humiliation, declares the Sovereign Lord."' (Ezekiel 16:59-63)*

Although I had broken my promise to him and deserved his punishment, God would not break his promises. If the people turned back to him, he would again forgive them and renew his covenant. He will not break his promise to give us salvation and forgiveness if we repent. The key here is the covenant (contract), he is a contract keeper, promise keeper if we confess our sins and turn away from them.

This would be the last time I ever resorted to that lifestyle again. I truly hit bottom when God slammed the door in my face. Everything that ever mattered to me, I realized now, I was losing. It takes losing everything worthwhile in life, severe consequences, to break the defiant, strong-willed, and rebellious.

This wasn't a life of faith or trust at all. Not of honesty or purity either. I wasn't living a spiritually principled life at all. God was sick of it; he was done with it! And so was my sponsor, and so was I.

Colossians 1:14 describes us as being redeemed as a slave is released. This redemption is nothing less than the forgiveness of sins. God completely destroyed the city of Sodom for its wickedness (see Genesis 24). It is a symbol of total destruction caused by wickedness. Similarly, nations containing cities with churches on every corner and Bibles in every home will have no excuse on judgment day if they do not repent and believe. God will destroy each for it's evil. The people of Bethesda, Korazin, and Capernaum saw Jesus first hand, and yet they stubbornly refused to repent of their sins and believe in him. It is worse to know the truth and not heed than to never know.

In the story of Sodom and Gomorrah, we see two facets of God's character—his great patience agreeing to spare a wicked city for ten good people and his fierce anger destroying both cities. As we grow spiritually, we should find ourselves developing not only a deeper respect for God because of his anger toward sin, but also a deeper love for God because of his patience when we sin. I realize now, through dreams, visions, and refusal to accept immoral behavior, exercising truth in love was God's warning to me before destruction. I need to call my sin what God says it is. I need to align myself with truth. I cannot make my will, wants, rationalizations, and justifications acceptable in comparison to God's truth or holiness. I need to call my conduct what God calls it.

> *Do you not know that your bodies are members of Christ himself? Shall I then take the members of Christ and unite them with a prostitute? Never! Do you not know that he who unites himself with a prostitute is one with her in body? For it is said, "The two will become one flesh." But whoever is united with the Lord is one with him in spirit. Flee from sexual immorality. All other sins a person commits is outside the body, but whoever sins sexually, sins against their own body. Do you not know that your bodies are temples of the Holy Spirit, who is in you, whom you have received from God? You are not your own; you were bought at a price. Therefore honor God with your bodies. (I Corinthians 6:15-20)*

Chapter 5

Big Faith

Understanding sin and forgiveness is a powerful lesson in God's mercy, grace, and loving-kindness toward us. Also, to pray and not give up, joining together with the righteous in prayer and supplication petitioning to God day and night. Our prayers are powerful, effective, and believing he hears and answers us.

This was an unexplained phenomenal act of God. I was slowly being awakened to His answer to my cry. I experienced his mercy and redemption in my darkest hour. I'm forever grateful for His deliverance.

I waited patiently for the Lord; he turned to me and heard my cry. He lifted me out of the slimy pit, out of the mud and mire; he set my feet on a rock and gave me a firm place to stand. He put a new song in my mouth, a hymn of praise to our God. Many will see and fear the Lord and put their trust in him. Blessed is the one who trusts in the Lord, who does not look to the proud, to those who turn aside to false gods. Many, Lord my God, are the wonders you have done, the things you planned for us. None can compare with you; were I to speak and tell of your deeds, they would be too many to declare. (Psalm 40:1-5)

Do not withhold your mercy from me, Lord; may your love and faithfulness always protect me. For troubles without number surround me; my sins have overtaken me, and I cannot see. They are more than the hairs of my head, and my heart fails within me. Be pleased to save me, Lord; come quickly, Lord, to help me. (Psalms 40:11-13)

David, the Psalmist, acknowledged that his sin caused his trouble. However, he experienced God's help in times of trouble, and this experience moved him to praise and greater faith. That has been the case with believers throughout history.

Prayer: Sins that burden me have overtaken me. I acknowledge judgment for my sin. I deserve God's wrath, yet in this circumstance, I was moved with deep conviction and obligation to live my life for you Lord, because of your loving-kindness and grace. I have received mercy, which I didn't deserve, but you chose to rescue, protect, and deliver me from sin, and reunite me with this animal I so dearly loved. This ostentatious event would be one of many divine situations leading me to repentance and being intentional to fully committing my ways to you, God. One hundred percent surrendered.

The Car

When I finally returned home, I intended to obtain legitimate employment. Temporarily, I was living at home with my parents until I found work and a place of my own. I went to temp agencies to headhunt for me as I had done previously in Oregon. I did get a job working in manufacturing plastics at a local major beverage company. It was extremely busy, working up to 60 hours a week at my first job. Money wasn't an issue, and I worked five and a half weeks without a day off. All I did was go to meetings and work.

I moved into a small studio near the college and local bus routes, which made transportation simple and getting to meetings and work accessible.

Due to exhaustion and imbalance due to an excessive work schedule, I put my notice in at this job for fear of relapsing. I then took employment elsewhere in manufacturing forty hours a week Monday through Thursday and went back to a salon on Friday and Saturday and occasionally did some catering in the evenings.

Seventeen years ago during, my first success at long term sobriety, I obtained two licenses in the nail and esthetics field. I always paid the annual fees for these two licenses during addiction, knowing there would come a time when I would return to legitimacy and sobriety. Thankfully this moment had arrived.

I was working two to three menial jobs to earn an honest living, haggling buses and rides daily for two and a half years. I was also paying off court fines for the reinstatement of my Driver's License. What a grueling process! Constantly, I would spend whatever extra money I had put aside from living expenses to pay these fines.

Finally, when this debt was paid in full, I had a license but couldn't afford a car, let alone insurance. Within a few months, I purchased a scooter, because it was all I could afford, and at least it was transportation. Riding this scooter was extremely difficult with harsh weather conditions from burning sun to rain that made it impossible to see, and then drain into the gas tank flooding it, making it stall and not driveable. Ultimately, I ended up pushing it home on several occasions. Exhausted, disgruntled, and extremely frustrated, I did not want to endure this much longer.

With my savings and help from my parents, I finally bought a one-owner vehicle with low mileage from a recent widow. My father, being a local pastor, knew a lot of people through his church, and when they put the word out, it wasn't long before we discovered a car. Because of the relationship with my parents, I purchased it at a fair price.

I could not believe this was even taking place. I was going to get behind the wheel again and drive! What used to take half a day by bus took an hour with the car. I was able to reciprocate, giving rides for people in recovery without transportation. What had so generously been done for me, I was able to reciprocate. This car was a gift from God, as well as my discipline, perseverance, and reaping a reward!

One evening in bed, a horrific crash occurred outside. It was a violent crash, springing my female next-door neighbor and me out of bed! She frantically ran outside asking if I had heard anything? I asked her, "What was that?" Moving to the front of my apartment where my car was parked, all the glass was broken in the back window, and a large tree branch was on top of my car.

I was broken, completely destroyed. Covering the car with a tarp to prevent further damage, I cried to God and proceeded with damage control the next morning.

Having AAA, I was able to have the car towed for an estimate of the damage and contacted my landlord for him to file a claim with his insurance company. He was resistant to any help, saying it was my responsibility. This compounded my hopelessness and despair. For days at work, I discussed this matter with co-workers as well as clients in desperation, seeking advice because I was completely confused and overwhelmed, not knowing how to take action.

My female neighbor helped remind me that the trees on the property were not maintained. Six months before this incident, her roof was caved in with a branch from the same tree. This was certainly negligence. Our landlord was asked to attend the maintenance of these dead branches, yet he neglected to do so.

Equiped with some confidence, I had another conversation with our landlord when he said it was an act of God. I replied, "a bolt of lightning is an act of God. This is negligence."

When he wouldn't budge, I was even more distraught. I constantly fretted and vented everywhere, every day to everyone. I didn't know what to do. I felt hopeless and helpless. Praying to God but not sure what to expect in return from Him. After all, I had "little faith."

Attending a small group at my local church, the group leader asked how I was doing. I broke down and wept, telling her I wanted to give up. When she asked why, I stated: "My car was totaled, that's why!" She replied, "Oh, that's too big for God..."

Puzzled? I didn't even realize or comprehend this is a problem God can and will absolutely solve.

I was under the assumption still if something were to happen, I had to make it happen as I always have. If I wanted or needed something, get busy, get it done—get into action. I never understood God's faithfulness, power, and sovereignty. Almost three years sober and full of fear and unbelief.

My sister and I had a conversation, and again I communicated how I wanted to give up. A person can only take so much!! She replied, "I can see those demons on that branch saying, 'yeah, this will really do her in' laughing at my suffering in hopes that one might fall."

Even then, puzzled... Demons... Could they really do this?

Not understanding spiritual warfare and the reality of demonic influences, I had so much to learn about struggles, testing, demonic warfare, and so much more to learn about God. He was allowing all of this though it didn't feel like it at the time for my development and an increase in faith. I felt disregarded, abandoned, neglected, utterly forsaken, and hopeless.

A client who worked for a law firm gave me some advice on how to get results. I acted quickly on her suggestion to get a copy of my lease and have a lawyer send him a certified letter. When I did this, he knew I was serious and about to take him to court. Then and only then, did he file a claim with his insurance company. He had never called in the first place, hoping I would foot the expense and merely go away. While all this was going on, I went through a process with his insurance company. They took depositions with my neighbor and I as well as multiple photos.

In fear that I might not get awarded compensation, I also asked the associate pastor on my way into worship one Sunday morning to pray for me concerning this case. He joined hands with me right on the spot, promptly praying. I was amazed at people acting and joining in prayer publicly without hesitation. This was all teaching me more about joining in faith, intercessory prayer, and believing, trusting, and waiting for God to act. I did wait, I did hope, and God did act.

I was awarded the insurance money that at least afforded me another car. Although I was not completely firm in the outcome, I hoped and prayed, pleading to God and did not give up. Lesson after lesson has been so necessary for my faith. I have since realized that without resistance, there is little development, and this was what was taking place.

Consider it pure joy, my brothers and sisters, whenever you face trials of many kinds, because you know that the testing of your faith produces perseverance. Let perseverance finish its work so that you may be mature and complete, not lacking anything. (James 1:2-4)

We don't really know the depth of our character until we see how we react under pressure. God wants to make us mature and complete. (Chronological Study Bible)

God blesses those who endure testing and temptation. Afterward they will receive the crown of life that God has promised to those who love them. (see James 1:12)

I endured a lot of hardships working manual labor and public transportation. I endured whatever was necessary to be honest, have integrity, disciplining myself with money and being utterly devoted to God. Looking back, I can see I was like a soldier in training, just suiting up doing what was mandatory to stay clean, serving God and surviving

The wisdom from God relates to life even during the most trying times. It is not a wisdom isolated from suffering and trials. This wisdom is the tool by which trials are overcome. The wise person chooses the most likely reason and proceeds to take action. This was a season of pressure and trials. Looking back, I don't know how I ever endured. God's grace, interruptions, and interventions is the only explanation. (James 1:5 – Chronological Study Bible)

The Apartment

Living in the same apartment, new neighbors moved in on the other side of the adjoining wall. As soon as my landlord left for Germany, as he did every summer, I noticed a pungent odor seeping through the walls and air conditioning system. The odor was so strong as well as chemical-smelling, it woke me in the evenings and kept me up all night. I spoke with the new tenants about my concern of this illicit drug odor and informed them of my abstinence involving drugs. They assured me there wasn't anything illegal occurring. This tenant informed me he was a painter, which explained the smell.

Satisfied for the moment, I let it go. When I returned home after an evening shift, I found it to be recurring, and the smell intensified. I then called law enforcement, and they weren't helpful. Not having any tangible evidence, there wasn't anything that could be done. I emailed my landlord about this and made a police report. Not wanting to expose my animals to this chemical that would inevitably kill them or expose myself to illicit substances, I had to take action–but how? What was to be done, and how to go about the process?

After law enforcement was called out again, a female officer noticed there wasn't any furniture at all in the apartment. I spoke with another officer seeking council. He said, "you know, and I know drug use is occurring, but again unless we have tangible evidence, we cannot obtain a search warrant."

Our hands were tied. After calling the police out on multiple occasions, I feared for my safety and my animals' safety. After all, I was bringing the heat down on them and interfering with their drug use as well as their manufacturing and profit. I vacated the premises with my cats going to my parents' house. They were away on vacation, allowing me a perfect opportunity to have my animals there without my dad's opposition. I could not risk their safety or jeopardize my recovery by tolerating this another minute.

Being removed from the toxicity for a couple of days, I needed to return home to gather a few things. I re-evaluated my circumstances. Perhaps I was overreacting, making more out of it than there was. After all, can I really trust my perceptions or my instincts? Doubting myself, I just wasn't sure. Before I went back, I knew to pray, to seek God's counsel. I asked ever so specifically, "Lord, if this is really you, wanting me to leave, let it be clear as a bell to me. If this is going on and dangerous for me to remain, let it be transparent what I am to do. Help me, show me; I need you, and I need you now!

When I opened the door to enter, I was actually blown backward from the chemical, and I heard

His voice ever so clearly say "Get Out." That was it! I was gone!! I got a couple of friends with a truck and moved everything I owned out of there and into my parent's patio within a few hours. Through all of this, I was grateful I had help to move, a safe place to move to, and at the time, my parents were out of state, making this transition less complicated. Here I was again in a transitional period, living at home with my parents.

As it says in James 1:4, these opportunities or trials, difficulties, and testing that I was enduring were training me to draw close to God. Clinging to Him for protection and staying close to Him for supernatural deliverance, I asked for clarity and wisdom, and he spoke to me. Not sure at the time where I was going to end up, how I was going to get there, but when I heard "get out," I knew God wanted me out that very instant. I listened to His voice, received instruction by faith, and acted on it.

I was asking Him to solve my problems, knowing what he had already done for me with Glouster and the car. This was all a whirlwind, but I stayed close to God, keeping Him as my number one priority. I then waited patiently for Him to act on my behalf.

While living with my parents, the entire time I was smack dab in the middle of the living room on their sofa bed. This wasn't my idea of comfort or privacy, but it was shelter and safety for my animals and me.

Weeks passed, then one morning on my way to work at the salon, I parked parallel on the street downtown. I was crossing to access the entrance of my workplace when an acquaintance crossed the street as well. When I told her about my present living situation, she enlightened me about her desire to move out of her apartment to pursue moving in with her boyfriend. Her apartment had two levels, a loft upstairs, and a downstairs. Her massage studio was on the ground level and her living quarters upstairs. One unit was very large with two bedrooms and two full baths. When she showed me her apartment, I was taken aback at the size and beautiful brick walls with vaulted ceilings in a brownstone building.

Not to mention, the location was diagonal across the street from my job! To her, this was a perfect fit being that I am an esthetician. Therefore, I would be respectful of her business underneath and understanding and courteous of noise. This was like a dream come true for me. I had wished to live in a brownstone building since I visited industrial cities. Now it was becoming a reality for me.

This in-fact became my apartment, the rent was cheaper, and the utilities were included. Furniture had been given to me, and I walked across the street daily to work. This was divinely orchestrated by God. When I finally moved in, I fell to my knees worshiping and praising God in awe, amazement, and adoration. I finally grasped His care and intimate detail with my life. At that moment, my faith entered a whole new dimension. I was awestruck about all that God had provided and done for me. I would never be the same. I could never doubt His power again. The evidence was overwhelming. I was in line with God; therefore, he was aligning things for me.

Thank You God, I am indebted to You. These things taking place have shaped my faith and trust in You.

> *Now all glory to God, who is able, through his mighty power at work within us, to accomplish infinitely more than we might ask or think. (Ephesians 3:20)*
>
> *And we know that in all things God works for the good of those who love him, who have been called according to his purpose. (Rom. 8:28)*

Study Notes – God works in everything, not just isolated incidents for our good. Evil is prevalent in our fallen world, but God can turn every circumstance around for our long-range good. Note that God is not working to make us happy but to fulfill his purpose.

As things went from bad to worse, I held on for dear life. Never really understanding how this could be for my benefit. But a transformation had already occurred within me so that I loved God, obeyed Him, and pursued him with all that I had. This is exactly the reason this promise was unfolding for me because no, I'm not perfect, but I love the Lord with all my heart, soul, and might, and absolutely nothing was going to come before this for me.

A Cure for Hepatitis C

God has performed so many miracles for me during my life that I could write a small book on these alone. The few mentioned in this book were the most applicable and powerful at this phase of my journey of stretching and developing my faith.

During my addiction, I contracted Hep-C by sharing an infected person's syringe. Early on, when I began to face some of the wreckage financially, relationally, and physically, I got a full panel of blood tests at the local health department and made the discovery. Of course, I was upset but accepted the fact this was unchangeable, therefore not curable.

Moving forward, after a couple of years clean, I did acquire healthcare through Obamacare and dealt with mild, first stage skin cancer. I was able to get an internal disease specialist who would be the doctor to guide me through Harvoni drug treatment that cures Hepatitis C.

Still being unsure and disbelieving, I could even acquire assistance; I applied to get pharmaceutical assistance only to be denied. Because of financial restraints, I could not afford the medication. The cost was one thousand dollars a month with insurance, outrageous and unattainable for me. I tried explaining my situation. There was a program available if, in fact, I qualified—Aetna Specialty pharmacy.

I prayed and lifted every anxiety and worry up to Jesus. I cast my cares on him because, after all, I knew now how much he cared for me. I dealt with a lot of bureaucracy through this process. Being organized, I began with paperwork, appointments, and payments to initiate the process. This was all part of functioning as a "normal," productive member of society. I was not used to doing any of this. I stayed calm and followed directions during the enrollment process. Even though I was insecure and believing I deserved so little, I walked by faith, believing and hoping God would take pity on me in my desperate time of need.

Going through channels of red tape always made me uncomfortable. Doubting myself and hiding a lot of shame, I thought, "If they knew me, they would reject me. If they knew the things I've done, they would discard me."

I believed the lies about myself and my value being connected with my abilities, performance, and past failures, even though I thought these things and to some extent, believed them, I carried on as though I didn't. I kept my thoughts to myself, closed my mouth, and moved my feet forward until I was approved and got results. Again, God showed up for me and gave me access to a solution to be cured and healthy.

From this point forward, I would be in a spiritual battle of cowardliness to confidence, fear to faith, and renewing my mind with the truth of God's word to produce a victorious emotion, action, and result. I had a realization, "no one knows what we have done unless you tell them." Revelations like, "people can't read your mind, Lisa." Good thing! LOL, Your past doesn't determine your future. You are not who you were–you are a new creation in Christ. A dearly loved, received, accepted, chosen child of God. Completely forgiven, the old has been erased for his sake. I am bought with a price, justified, purified, and sanctified. Realizing being aligned with God in His will produces amazing outcomes. "Anything is possible with God" and realizing how much self-defeating, self-sabotaging, actions I take that delay my destiny. How much the enemy lies and whispers to my deepest fears and deepest wounds of unworthiness, rejection, and abandonment.

If I remain unworthy, I won't pursue anything because, ultimately, I don't deserve it. There's a sense of "dirty shame" for all the things I've done as if I'm not fully forgiven. If I'm not fully forgiven, I'm held in bondage and in guilt of my sin. If I am in bondage with shame, I will never be open to receive God's gifts or goodness that he wants to pour out on me. I'm not as good as everyone else—"normal," therefore comparing cultivating separation. People who have kept a certain standard are first in line for a benefit. People like me are undeserving. God couldn't really love someone as damaged or broken as me? Could He?

Believing these lies keeps me isolated, withdrawn, set apart, disunited from others and ultimately from God. All my thoughts of unworthiness and self-doubt about my place in this world almost feels as if everyone sees right through me and knows what I am thinking or feeling—a constant preoccupation with self. I'm not much, but I'm all I think about.

Because of feelings of irrelevance, it affects the way I cope in society and everyday relationships. If I listen to these lies and whispers long enough without an anchor of truth and light, I am doomed to break, give up, sabotage myself and my efforts, and ultimately check out, numb out, or go insane. Thank God for my church, wise counsel, my sponsor, and her guidance. The word of God and prayer teaching me through all these moments of insanity and delusion. Through self-examination, repentance, and prayer, God was bringing me out of darkness into the light. My spirit through the union of the Holy Spirit was awakening at the war raging within me. How critical, judgmental, and condemning I was of myself and others.

> *For he has rescued us from the dominion of darkness and brought us into the kingdom of the Son he loves… (Colossians 1:13)*
>
> *We demolish arguments and every pretension that sets itself up against the knowledge of God, and we take captive every thought to make it obedient to Christ. (2 Corinthians 10:5)*
>
> *Take the helmet of salvation and the sword of the Spirit, which is the word of God. (Ephesians 6:17)*

Remember, this battle must be fought in God's strength, depending on the word and God through prayer.

I was approved by this specialty pharmacy, and made all my doctor appointments, blood work, and everything that was required of me. One year later, after completion, I was virus-free. Deliverance by God again!

For now, this will be the closing of miracles from God, though he has continued and will continuously do even more because now I know that's who he is and what he does. He is my help in my time of crisis, the mere beginning of understanding God's love for me, help in need, always providing a way of escape, and unfolding His unwavering favor over me, proving time and time again, he rescues those he loves. I am learning, as time goes on, how valuable I am to my loving Father God, not based on anything I could earn. His love is unconditional because I am his daughter. his dearly loved child, nothing more!

Chapter 6

Building a Life

Do not conform to the pattern of this world, but be transformed by the renewing of your mind. Then you will be able to test and approve what God's will is—his good, pleasing and perfect will. (Romans 12:2)

At this time of my recovery and walk with God, I was ingesting God's word daily. Truth was replacing old thoughts about myself, and unworthiness into the assurance of God's presence, and courage were prevalent, allowing me to do things I never imagined possible before. Living in my glorious new apartment, part of my lease responsibilities was managing the building and parking lot. I was responsible for fire inspections, fire alarm, and checking with the fire department if alarm problems occurred, as well as employee parking.

Brownstone Apartment / Parking Lot Issues

My residence and the massage therapist were at one end of the building, and several art studios were upstairs, with restaurants, a bar, and a tattoo parlor below on the other side of the building.

I began to notice issues with improper and excessive business/employee parking. Still being unsure of myself and all the facts, I was reluctant to approach the store owners. I was afraid of making too much out of this, overacting or not assuming full responsibility for my duties, again wavering in self-doubt, which was it? And if these parking limits were violations, who do I approach first and how do I go about it? I knew to confront this meant going down to a couple of pubs, restaurants, and a tattoo parlor, which were all friends, a camaraderie, a "brotherhood." Being up against this intensified my fear. If I were to persist, this "brotherhood" would link arms, and I alone would be confronting an army.

Upstairs in my apartment, I was tossing all of this around in my mind. Satin's lies would tell me this

Imaginations to Revelations

is too big for me, not penetrable. Here was a scared straight girl new on the scene having no merit or weight. What will become of me if I am outwitted, outnumbered, and overpowered?

Breathing deeply, inviting God's presence into this situation, His word came to me and His wisdom on how to orchestrate order. An awakening revelation occurred. "If God didn't think I was equipped to handle this, he wouldn't have given me this apartment nor the responsibility. Do you suppose God knows what he's doing?"

His words clearly came to me. Of course, he does. He doesn't make mistakes. If I didn't belong, I wouldn't be here.

> *For the Spirit God gave us does not make us timid, but gives us power, love and self-discipline. (2 Timothy 1:7)*

> *But my righteous one will live by faith. And I take no pleasure in the one who shrinks back. (Hebrews 10:38)*

That was it! I had to walk by faith, act courageously, and God showed me how. Also, I couldn't fathom God not being pleased with me. Immediately, I went downstairs. I approached delicately, asked probing questions about their cars. Since two cars per establishment were the limit, this would be my footing for finding out each person's car, and when more than two were parked, that would be the evidence needed to establish exceeding maximum capacity. In doing so, they were, in fact, in error. I politely asked for them to correct this.

When the facts were laid out, there was no disputing, and when approached diplomatically and being gentle in warning them, I then had grounds if repeated to go to my supervisor for a written letter to be drawn up, taking it out of my hands. This was difficult for me being the new kid on the block, not to mention walking into bars and a tattoo parlor being abstinent from drugs and alcohol. I had God's spirit and power living in me, his presence walking beside me, and his voice prompting and ordering me exactly the way to go. After obeying his voice and walking in this direction, I was relieved, empowered, and growing in faith, courage, and wisdom.

> *Blessed are you, Israel! Who is like you, a people saved by the Lord? He is your shield and helper and your glorious sword. Your enemies will cower before you, and you will tread on their heights. (Deuteronomy 33:29)*

Fear of man will prove to be a snare, but whoever trusts in the Lord is kept safe. (Proverbs 29:25)

Because God will examine what kind of workers we have been for him, we should build our lives on His word and build His word into our lives. It alone tells us how to live for him and how to serve him. Believers who ignore the Bible will certainly be ashamed at the judgment. Consistent and diligent study of God's word is vital otherwise we will be lulled into neglecting God and our true purpose for living. (Chronological Study Bible 2 Tim. 2:15)

Frankie – Letting Go

My ex-boyfriend finally got off heroin and was on methadone. He began cleaning up his life and then creeping back into mine. Phone calls were increasing, and when we talked, I sensed his wanting me back into his life. I had been single and celibate for a couple of years at the time and was completely focused on my relationship with God and work. Independently sustaining my life was freeing and satisfying. I was alone but not lonely. I had solitude instead of boredom.

Our levels of maturity were far apart. By the time he got off street drugs and began to crawl in diapers, I was in middle school. I sensed a great gap in maturity and knowledge of God. He would speak to me (in myths) of the Nephilim and Enoch. Always bringing up these old myths instead of how applicable scripture is now, molding our values, standards, and beliefs. He would discuss things with me about "working the system" that would disturb me, knowing a principled life is a Godly life. I sought honesty, integrity, purity, selflessness rather than dishonesty, scheming, hustling, sexual immorality, and greed.

When he would converse sexually on the phone, I became extremely uncomfortable, understanding if I responded, verbally condoning or partnering in this way, he had ownership and another "ticket or free ride" financially. Again, unsure of the way to completely sever this relationship, I avoided him. One day it was becoming obvious to him something was wrong. I went to work asking God to intervene, for if he didn't, I wouldn't know how to communicate this need to move on. "God, if you don't intervene, I don't know what to do. If you don't help me, I'm doomed, despaired, defeated, forsaken."

In so many ways in my feeble attempts, I was asking for wisdom and interceding power. James 1:5 tells us that if you ask for wisdom, God will give it generously without finding fault.

If any of you lacks wisdom, he should ask God who gives generously to all without finding fault and it will be given to him. (James 1:5)

Something was transpiring within me knowing as I grew in God's knowledge, abiding in Him, and remaining in His love, I did not want the things I used to want. My desires were changing. My eyes were open to reality and truth. I wasn't dependent or addicted to Frankie anymore. He didn't have the same power over me as he once had. God had power over me, not Frankie.

When he was flirtatious and sexual in conversation, I felt dirty, disgust, and shame. I was clean, living in obedience to God's word, being sexually pure for the first time, and I didn't want to compromise for anyone. I didn't want to trade in God's miraculous provision for sin. I wanted to honor him in body and deeds. Honoring God was my utmost priority—honoring him with my body, my soul, and my life.

When Frankie did call, God intervened. He asked," Do you love me anymore?"

I remained silent, not uttering a word because I couldn't honestly answer him. He replied, "your silence has told me everything."

Therefore knowing, I no longer loved him or wanted anything that we once had again. God took care of things, being aligned with Him and obedient, praying, and asking for help. Finally, this relationship was completely severed, and I was delivered completely set free.

Sponsorship

As I was deepening my knowledge of God as well as strengthening my relationship, I had a strong desire to serve others. Being indebted to God for all he has done for me, I was compelled to use my gifts, talents, and abilities to serve others. Understanding Jesus was the King of Kings who came to serve motivated me to want the same thing.

> *Each of you should use whatever gift you have received to serve others, as faithful stewards of God's grace in its various forms. If anyone speaks, they should do so as one who speaks the very words of God. If anyone serves, they should do so with the strength God provides, so that in all things God may be praised through Jesus Christ. To him be the glory and the power for ever and ever. (1 Peter 4:10-11)*

Everyone has gifts. Find yours and use them. When we use them as he directs us to help others, they will see Jesus in us, and glorify Him for the help they have received. I began working with other women in recovery, mentoring them through a 12-step workbook, speaking at meetings, speaking in jails and other institutions. Pouring into others helped me practice what I was preaching. I certainly wasn't going to give direction or guidance hypocritically. Finally, I was able to take my painful and shameful past and turn it into a valuable asset. Having firsthand experience to understand someone's plight in life, along with a solution through victory in Christ, was unparalleled.

I began to recognize that helping others was a privilege, as well as a responsibility. This service was changing my confidence and fulfilling a sense of purpose for my life. Along with so many benefits, this also came with disadvantages. I had no idea the magnitude of abandonment and rejection I still felt when these women were relapsing on drugs or alcohol, getting into relationships moving upward and onward; thus, no longer needing me anymore. Ouch! This one hurt! When they were without transportation and no outlet from their community living, I was on the top priority list. When they got a vehicle or a boyfriend this radically changed. I also realized that I was doing all the running and most of the work leaving me frustrated and depleted.

I remember one evening bringing a girl to hear a motivational speaker. I had already done so much for this woman. After being released from jail, I permitted her an overnight stay in my apartment, sacrificing time for phone calls. My investment in her was significant. When we arrived at this event, she mentioned she wanted to sit upfront. Not inviting me to join her, she just moved away, sat with others, leaving me to sit alone. Halfway through this event, I was not engaged and chose to leave. I left her there never to engage again. This was rude, disrespectful, and inconsiderate. I felt disregarded, discarded like a piece of trash. Her disrespect and discourteous behavior were painful as well as demeaning. I felt unappreciated and used.

Similar things in succession were happening from other women, and I had to evaluate my strategy. Obviously this approach was ineffective. I was foolishly burning up energy, time, and gas. I also had to evaluate my worth, my power or lack thereof.

EVALUATIONS

- What did I do to get clean and stay clean this time?
- I invested everything - one hundred %
- I did things if possible, without inconveniencing others
- I didn't avoid things that were difficult or painful for my benefit/ went to any length
- I was rigorously honest and had integrity
- I was willing to go to any length/endured hardship having discipline

I realized nothing ventured nothing gained. If I don't invest, there's no reward or dividend. I was investing more than they were and had burned out, becoming frustrated and angry. I then decided to step down from working with others in transitional living. I had to value my time and myself by cutting a clear boundary with the things that work and things that do not.

On a larger scale, I kept my speaking commitments and greeting at my church. I also had the opportunity to minister and pray with clientele who had family struggling with addiction, marital issues, or grieving the loss of a loved one. I was still pouring into others whenever, wherever a need was found, just in a different capacity. Scaling back was important to know what frustrates and exhausts me. Running myself ragged all over town being a taxi isn't helping maximize my potential. Therefore God wouldn't want me doing it.

During all these situations, I took solitude with God, pouring out my heart, my hurts, and my questions. Why? What do I do? I asked for wisdom, guidance, direction, clarity, peace, and healing. Understanding myself helps me know what is fulfilling and what is not. When these rejections happened, it forced me to do a lot of work around this area. My sponsor tells me when I am disturbed, I am wrong no matter what the cause. So, when I do an examination of my pain and sadness due to my rejections and nonacceptance by others, I have discovered an unhealthy dependence on others for validation, acceptance, and worth. These hobbling demands must be broken.

I demand the absolute control of situations, circumstances, and people for security, satisfaction, and worth. When these demands aren't met, I am left crippled, disappointed, and disillusioned.

I began to process these hurts through the God of comfort and compassion, falling at the foot of the cross with my suffering. Going to the place my savior suffered, to the one who understands suffering like no other. With him, I was met with great love and received mercy, grace, and understanding. I confess my anger, pride, and unforgiveness before him. In exchange, he gives me freedom from bondage, his peace, and undying love.

Instead of looking for a distraction in entertainment, relationships, or any other form of indulgence, I allowed myself to feel and grieve the pain rather than run from it. His gentle whispers assured me he chose me, loved me before I ever came to be. He has protected and guarded me my entire life. He was enlightening me that God was selecting and sanctifying me for something else. Something more deserving of me.

These relationships were for a season, not a lifetime. They were for me to understand through these rejections, to be more selective with what I am willing to give.

- Is what I am doing helping someone or enabling?
- Am I streamlining order and balance into my life, so I am full and refreshed?
- When I am full, I can pour into others
- When empty, I leave myself drained and deprived

These are lessons that I have developed to help me be a peaceful, balanced, confidant person, better equipped to serve. Also becoming more efficient and wiser with planning and decision making.

Chapter 7

Breaking Financial Strongholds

My entire time clean, I was working in manufacturing and catering for temp services. Initially, the plan was to get back into my career, nails and aesthetics, only on weekends. As time progressed, I transitioned into the salon full time during the day, catering only periodically. When I focused only on my career after about five years sober, I began struggling financially. Completely dependent on client-based sustenance, I was having car trouble multiple times, taking it to my mechanic. A flat tire and the spare was also defective, and I had to ride home on the rim.

Soon after, my equipment at work broke down, forcing me to send it in for repair, and when the distributor received the machine, it was irreparable. I was forced to purchase a new machine since this was the largest source of my revenue. Until the new one was delivered, I was unable to provide the service, drastically affecting my income. All of these monetary crises were simultaneous, compounding my stress and despair.

Looking back, I now see I was being tested by God to assess my faithfulness and commitment to remain firm in faith, pure in thought, word, and deed. I hate to admit my lack thereof. Unlike Job enduring under intense suffering, never denouncing God, I wasn't able to withstand this suffering for long. Simultaneously, things went from bad to worse, driving me to anger, rage, defiance, rebellion, and ending in denouncing God.

I would love to tell you I was rooted and established in the faith, unwavering after all God had done for me, but I fell apart. I became so angry with God. I raised my fist and voice at Him. In disgust, I couldn't believe he was allowing this to take place! After all I was a faithful steward of my time and service, helping women, speaking in institutions, faithful with my tithe and charitable donations. Look how much I do, look how much I give! How dare you allow me to endure this type of hardship and suffering, when I've given of my life, time, talents, services,

Imaginations to Revelations 77

and resources to kingdom purposes. I knew God was a rewarder of those who walked and lived by faith, faithful to his promises, so why then Lord are you withholding from me? I didn't understand why he was allowing things to become so difficult for me without reprieve?

For the Lord disciplines those he loves (Hebrews 12:6)

Do not despise the Lord's discipline because he disciplines those he loves. (Proverbs 3:11-12)

I was anointed with oil at a small group meeting. I broke down and wept as they prayed over me to rebuke the spirit of lack and fear. I was emotionally and spiritually set free after that. I realize now that this hardship revealed a level of frustration and desperation, thoughts of resorting to prostitution to get out of debt. After all this time, how quickly I resorted to this method of thinking and operation. This was so entrenched in me it was still an option that only a dilemma of this magnitude would reveal.

In the Gospel of Matthew, Peter swore that he would never fall away from Jesus. Jesus responded that this very night, you will disown me three times (see Matthew 26:33-35). Peter stated that even if I have to die with you, I will never disown you. Like Peter, I too swore that I could never disown or denounce God, yet I did. Like Peter denying Christ, I am feeble and human. Also, like Peter, I was immersed in shame and self-loathing.

Feeling utterly worthless before God as if what I had done was, in a sense, unforgivable, like Peter, I was filled with remorse, sorrow, and condemnation. Of course, God restored Peter and later on this rock I will rebuild my church. God would also restore and rebuild me.

I took my car back to the mechanic, and he did not charge me for the repairs. What mechanic doesn't charge you? As I was waiting in the lobby while repairs were being made, a female mechanic who attends my church came up to me, remarking on my testimony I gave a few Sundays earlier and how it had touched her. Minding my own business, reading devotions while I waited, I never anticipated this girl I had never seen would encourage me.

You never know who is watching. God is over all, in all, and through all. Amazing! This would be one of many trials with money until I passed the test. During this financial upheaval, I couldn't possibly afford another machine, either. Another generous patient man was the distributor of the equipment.

Knowing my predicament, he agreed to send a replacement and for me to make payments. This allowed me to conduct services without interrupting revenue.

Though everything was collapsing, God was orchestrating things behind the scenes for my benefit. Miracles in the mess! Everything was a mess, but God was performing the supernatural, the miraculous! Still so much to learn. God separates the wheat from the chaff. When these pressures come, it reveals what is in my heart. My denouncing God and spewing curses was more than a speech problem, it was a heart problem. I've since learned, God is good, it is his nature and character. He is holy therefore pure and good. He allows the destroyer to work havoc, deliver a thorn, and do his dirty work. Since God cannot get his hands dirty, he delivers the thorn through the evil one. The test and pressure come from the outside, temptation from within.

After this test, I realized how far off the beam I got and how unspiritual I was, unlike Job. One of the biggest snares for me has always been money, either too much of it, gaining it immorally, or not enough of it. It has always represented a false sense of power and security. When I had it, I was powerful and secure; when I didn't, I was insignificant, insecure, and irrelevant. Being sober and responsible, I was frugal and disciplined with my earnings; my bills were paid, groceries and whatever was leftover went for business supplies and cat food. This comes straight from my journal: "I work so hard, I feel I am dog paddling to keep my head above water."

> *Lord, let your ear be attentive to the prayer of this your servant and to the prayer of your servants who delight in revering your name. Give your servant success today by granting him favor in the presence of this man. (Nehemiah 1:11)*

I began to present my need before the Lord. I began to pronounce his word over my circumstances. I began to repent of my worship, obsession, and worry of money or lack thereof. Every time a doubt or worry came into my mind, I would cast it down and denounce it as a lie, claiming my God-given rights as a believer and an heir to the throne. Through a lot of worship, podcast, bible studies, sermons, reading, and studying scripture, my knowledge of God grew, as well as my understanding of the truth regarding money.

To every promise there's a premise.

Give, and it will be give to you. A good measure, pressed down, shaken together and running over, will be poured into your lap. For with the measure you use, it will be measured to you. (Luke 6:38)

Those who trust in their riches will fall...(Proverbs 11:28)

Whoever gives to the poor will lack nothing, but those who close their eyes to poverty will be cursed. (Proverbs 28:17)

Bring all the tithes into the storehouse so there will be enough food in my house. If you do so says the Lord of heaven's armies, "I will open the windows of heaven for you. I will pour out such a blessing so great you won't have enough room to take it in! Try me put me to the test! (Malachi 3:10)

I was a good steward of my time, resources, and finances. I didn't wastefully spend or rack up credit card debt. I was obedient to God's commands and his instructions in his word; therefore instead of panicking, freaking out, and quitting internally, I needed to believe he would deliver me as he promises. It wasn't if God would act; it was when he would act. As I've already testified in previous pages, it is also my experience that he is the 11th hour God!

Another realization is that my words set my world in motion. Speaking curses, curses myself. Reaping and sowing were more than simply financial. I was speaking curses over myself without even realizing it. I was reaping all the negative I was uttering.

> *The tongue has the power of life and death, and those who love it will eat its fruit. (Proverbs 18:21)*

From this point forward, whenever issues with money would arise, I would never again handle it the same. I thought of many quick fixes, but never uttered anything contrary to God's word. My ex-boyfriend? Absolutely not. Other things came to mind as well, but instead of hanging onto them as before, I quickly made my thoughts agreeable and aligned them to the will of God.

> *Finally, brothers , whatever is true, noble, right, excellent, praiseworthy, lovely and admirable think about such things. (Philippians 4:8)*

Every painful occurrence has brought a defining, refining process to my life. The last episode of blaming and cursing God brought about a transformation, an awakening of God's goodness. It's not his fault. Instead of grumbling, venting, and complaining, I kept silent and had an internal shift that this recurring theme was necessary to bring forth a trust, confidence in God. An utter reliance in him alone, an unshakable belief in his word.

> *Better the little that the righteous have than the wealth of the wicked. For the power of the wicked will be broken but the Lord upholds the righteous. (Psalm 37:16-17)*

> *I will prevent pests from devouring your crops and the vines in your field will not cast their fruit says the Lord Almighty. Then all the nations will call you blessed for yours will be a delightful land says the Lord Almighty. (Malachi 3:11-12)*

While I was crawling like a snail and saw others surpass me in the workplace and elsewhere, I was painfully aware of my lack of business and resources, yet this time was not going to be any temporal or material fixes for relief or pleasure. Sustaining this spiritual discipline was brutal; all that remained was at the core, and that was not pretty. Unworthiness and financial insufficiency left me feeling desperate and broken. I began to lament as David did in the Psalms, pouring out my entire heart to God.

> *Come, all you who are thirsty, come to the waters; and you who have no money, come, buy and eat! Come, buy wine and milk without money and without cost. Why spend money on what is not bread, and your labor on what does not satisfy? Listen, listen to me, and eat what is good, and you will delight in the richest of fare. (Isaiah 55:1-2)*

My flesh was screaming. Dying to self is a grieving process, dying on the inside. Denial of acting out in any way, keeping my gaze before me, my spirit was experiencing a rebirth, being made alive in Christ. Knowing he alone is my source, provider, comfort, peace, and only hope. I stood firm on his promises of provision.

> *A hard worker has plenty of food but a person who chases fantasies ends up in poverty. (Proverbs 28:19)*

> *Wealth from get-rich quick schemes quickly disappears; wealth from hard work grows over time. Proverbs (13:11)*

> *For you O Lord will bless the righteous; With favor you will surround him with a shield. (Psalm 5:12)*

I started speaking life out loud, claiming daily truths, promises, and rewards about money. For thirty days, I prayed the prayer of Jabez, and God began to act. I began speaking truth and life over me and ate the fruit of it.

My business was exploding, new clients scheduling higher-end services, reaping a higher profit. I was grateful. As I have relayed my devotion to God during these pages, he is first not last. I honor him with my wealth and gifts. I do not want his hand without his face, nor the gift without the giver. I simply want God and to use what he has given me to further kingdom purposes. Enjoying the fruit of your labor is a gift from God, my priorities must be in order—God first.

Summing up how this and every lesson has changed me.

- His word has transforming power
- Speaking life gives life (life and death are in the power of the tongue)
- Knowing God is what he says he is
- Knowing and trusting that God fulfills his promises
- To seek, ask, and believe I receive

- Repent and forgive others, so prayers are unblocked
- Look beyond the pain to the lesson
- Putting God first and keep him first
- Reading and meditating on God's word keeps my thoughts pure and my heart secure

This type of prayer, affirmation, and walk of faith have changed my business, and it has changed me.

> *And when I ask I believe I will receive and that it is done for me. (Matthew 21:22)*

> *O Lord, the God of Israel there is no God like you in heaven or on earth, keeping your covenant of loving devotion with your servants who walk before you with all their hearts. (2 Chronicles 6:14)*

Chapter 8

Dating Danny

As I mentioned already, I lived disciplined and orderly in a daily routine. I worked five to six days a week, exercised regularly, kept service commitments, and worshiped on Sundays. Sunday was my day to worship God, regroup with domestic responsibilities, ending the day watching a movie to relax. One Sunday, while I was watching my typical movie, I thought out loud, "Is this all there is?"

I wondered at that precise moment, is there possibly more life could offer me? Not that I was dissatisfied with my life or present circumstances at all, not complaining, but I had been so focused on recovery, my church, and career, and had been consistent with this lifestyle for the past six and a half years. Quite frankly, it was necessary in the beginning to establish a firm foundation. I didn't have room for anything else.

For the first time, I was single and happy about it. I loved my job, my life, my freedom, living alone without any distractions. For the first time in my life, I was single, complete and fully free. As this thought came to my mind, "Is this all there is," I had a longing for more. Perhaps after all this time being able to focus only on getting healthy and being whole, I was beginning to consider the possibility of what life might be like if I were in a relationship? An inner prompting occurred that I had enough growth and maturity to engage in dating or be ready if, in fact, I met someone.

There were a couple of men who expressed interest, and the thought of dating any of them frightened me because of my commitment to purity. I felt as though I had to defend my moral values as well as my faith.

After much discussion with my sponsor, and a lot of inventory work, I came to the realization I wasn't free or secure in my position at all. I was guarded and defensive. I feared ridicule, persecution, and rejection. Part of me was ready, but at the same time, I was projecting scenarios about the future and the reaction of others when holding steadfast to biblical standards. Until now, I had a fortress built up around me that people could sense for miles. I gave distinct vibes of disinterest and disengagement. Men need not dare look or get close to me for they would be met with disapproval and rejection

Finally, I agreed to go to lunch with someone. Lunch is harmless, so I went. I was awakened to how nice it would be to have someone pick up the tab, court me, and have companionship. Since lunch went so well, I agreed to have dinner. After dinner with this individual, I discerned this was not an equivalent mate at all. I discerned danger through our conversation referring to pain management and sexual inappropriateness. I had enough self-respect and worth to determine what I wanted and excellent boundaries. Previously, I had none at all. This wasn't the man for me, and then I met another.

I was speaking at a recovery engagement, and the male speaker that evening would later be the next person I would date. And so it goes…dating Danny.

Our first dinner date went extremely well. The following morning, I was overwhelmed with emotion since I had never been treated so well. I actually cried over someone courting and treating me so respectfully. He treated me like a princess, and never had

I experienced this. My entire life I endured abuse, neglect, and rejection.

On our second date, we went to a concert. I hadn't been to a concert in decades. All this part of courting was fabulous! During the show, we shared binoculars, as he drew closer to me physically, becoming extremely suffocating and sexually oriented in conduct. I only wanted to hang out, dance, have fun, and get to know him better, yet as it continued, it made it impossible to relax. Instead of magnetizing me, it recoiled me. Later in the conversation, an overnight bag, massages, and mention of a spare room were discussed. Knowing where this was leading, this is something I wasn't even going to entertain nor visit. My response was no. The door is shut, slammed shut!!!

After dropping me home, a text came in the middle of the night regarding the spare room and overnight bag, mentioning I should change my mind and stay. I ignored the text. I had already expressed my deep convictions regarding sexual morality and marriage; touched briefly on my past and failed marriages. Of course, this has been pivotal in not wanting to repeat the same mistakes. He wasn't comprehending anything I said. He had his own desires and intentions; nothing I stated was detouring him. After this incident, I had a strong conviction I probably was going to have to stop seeing him.

All the fears of defending my convictions and my faith were unfolding in front of me, and God was allowing sifting and testing; I was steadfast in this decision, unmoved. Divinely the sermon that Sunday morning was on biblical standards in a hostile, rebellious world against God.

After all of this, I was ready to take a break and return to singlehood. I was determined to live for God, obey his word, and honor him. After everything God has done for me, I wasn't about to trade my relationship with him for anything in the world. Not for money, fame, or love. Either get on board or get out! Too much pain, heartache, and regret lie in all past relationships. I've had an awakening in this area due to failures and intense suffering. I was not about to repeat this again.

As I hit my knees that morning, I decided to break it off due to complete obligation and obedience to God. I was preparing to have this finality with him by phone. Instead, the phone call came to me. He made amends for his conduct, relaying to me God had come to him in a dream. During this dream, God convicted him of his harm to me. In his morning meditation, he was convicted of his selfishness, and he sincerely owned his mistakes with an apology.

At this moment, I was amazed that God was actually dealing with an enemy, convicting them of their disrespect, and supernaturally protecting me. When I prayed to God, I asked if there would be anyone who would honor me in this way. Petitioning God to bring a man who would honor me, and then the miraculous phone call came. Dan was enlightened of his errors, as well as the reality of losing me; I had to respect the humility and courage to take responsibility for wrong done and the honesty and willingness to clean it up. God was showing me again, and again, everything, everyone is under his sovereignty. He was still assuring me that he was attending to every detail concerning me.

Things proceeded with both of us. Spending a lot of time together, he cooked for me, fourth of July fireworks and movies. Working through building a friendship, keeping boundaries, enjoying companionship and courting, he asked for a commitment. Stating honestly, I told him I was only ready for friendship, nothing more. We went to another concert, sitting directly in front of someone who knew one of the performers. They asked me if I wanted to go on stage as a dancer. Most definitely! This was a once in a lifetime opportunity!

Despite Danny's opposition, I leaped for the opportunity! I was backstage, then on stage! Dancing several songs to the '80s, this was awesome for me. When I returned to my seat, Danny wasn't there. Instead of him being there, I was met by an attendee. All along, we were sitting in the wrong section. Getting called up to dance with a performing artist occurred by being in the wrong place at the wrong time. Wow! Unbelievable!

Unfortunately for Danny, he wasn't thrilled about this at all. He was extremely upset, actually jealous. We exchanged words on the way home, trying to explain myself; he was disappointed and hurt that I chose to go on stage instead of spending time with him. The next morning, he broke up with me, explaining he'd rather deal with the pain than stay involved with someone not in love with him. Keeping in mind, this was only our fourth or fifth date. This would be a pattern over the next several months; on again, off, up, down, all around. A bit of a rollercoaster. Prior to this, all past relationships were boy meets girl, immediately physical as well as sexual, then moving in together.

I had no idea what I was doing or what I wanted; after all, I had not been on a date since I was a teenager a couple of times. Even as a teen, everything I pursued was purely physical and sexual, thinking that was the only way to gain acceptance, adoration, validation, and some type of love.

Meanwhile, he agreed to go to my non-denominational worship, forsaking his catholic practices. We attended church together. Things were moving forward rapidly, getting serious with talk of marriage. Primarily my waiting to commit was the fear of him holding out, abstaining sexually. I knew he was abstaining for me, not so much for God. Knowing full well, if I had given him permission, he would have definitely proceeded.

We began preparing for our future. One worship service I attended alone, a fellow church member ran across the sanctuary to warn me about a dream from God. Strongly suggesting I wasn't listening or in a position to listen. So many warnings internally and through a couple of different individuals expressing this dream and concern of this may not be the right man, or just not the right time.

The further plans progressed toward moving out of my apartment into his condo one town over. I began to realize what I was giving up—privacy, independence, my own apartment, walking distance to work. The many amazing benefits turned to panic and uncertainty.

I reflected on both my failed marriages, both being doomed by drug addiction and infidelity. My second marriage was a mistake from the beginning. Meeting in early recovery, immediately engaging sexually, and living together. So many doubts about the relationship, yet married anyway. What was I thinking?

I was afraid of hurting him and stayed because of convenience and pity. The marriage ended in infidelity, relapse, and heartache. I was a horrible wife; he had his own issues. Our union was built on sand. I had so many promptings yet ignored them. This was one of the most painful regrets of my life; therefore, I wasn't about to let another similar instance occur. I put on the brakes and told Danny the truth; I wasn't ready. Quite frankly, I was scared to death. We continued dating, but something shifted internally for me, and our relationship was not the same.

Chapter 9

Humiliations Before Humility

During this season of my life, I also was in a leadership group, and I divulged confidential information. (To honor the relationship, I will not divulge anything further.) My heart, in doing so, was to defend and restore someone's reputation. Nevertheless, I broke confidentiality and was wrong. The mistreatment and slander of this individual disturbed me to the core. Therefore I couldn't let it go, which exacerbated the situation. I was pulled aside in confidence and put on probation from leadership.

A gossip betrays confidence a trustworthy man keeps a secret. (Proverbs 10:13)

Do not be quick with your mouth, do not be hasty in your heart to utter anything before God. God is in heaven and you are on earth, so let your words be few. (Ecclesiastes 5:2)

Following this conversation, I didn't respond well. For some time, I felt minimized, and there was favoritism. Being insecure, this only magnified doubt, inferiority, rejection, and imaginations. Feeling others were welcomed with proclamation, and my presence and input somehow was an irritant, this was an emotional recipe for disaster. When this confrontation occurred, I unleashed with a fury! I unloaded and exploded everything I was harboring onto this individual without a healthy channel of process. I was crushed regarding this removal and was projecting and inflicting it upon them.

I wept for days, agonizing, and humiliated. Consumed with anguish, wrath, rage, and malice, I wanted to give up. Simultaneously, an incident happened at my workplace. Being disgruntled, wreaking with fury and despair from within, unable to pretend, it was also leaking out onto clients and co-workers.

A lovely elderly client gave me a candy bar, and I placed it rudely with community candy right in front of her. Making this client uncomfortable, as well as offended, she no longer wanted me performing services for her and asked a co-worker to do so in the future. Emotionally, I was spiraling into a pit of darkness and despair. All I could do was weep before the Lord day and night. Weeping and grieving this loss was excruciating like a death. After all, I was dying, feeling as if I was being thrown away, rejected as my deepest wound now being brought to light.

> *Hear my voice when I call O Lord be merciful to me and answer me. My heart says to you seek his face, your face Lord I will seek. (Psalm 27:7)*

I was crying out for mercy, seeking him, his face, his justice and an answer to my cries.

> *Do not hide your face from me. Do not turn your servant away in anger. You have been my helper. Do not reject me or forsake me O God my savior. (Psalm 27:9)*

Being so desperate for God to come quickly to me, feeling rejected and forsaken by leaders and clients, I couldn't bear the possibility of being forsaken by God.

> *Though my mother and father forsake me the Lord will receive me. (Psalm 27:10)*

There was a comfort in seeking and lamenting to the Lord. A release and relief from pain and heartache.

> *Teach me your way O Lord lead me down the right path because of my oppressors. Do not turn me over to the desire of my foes for false witness may rise up against me. I am still confident of this, I will still see the goodness of the Lord in the land of the living. (Psalm 27:11-13)*

Like David, I felt misunderstood, reviled, despised, whether fancied or real. It seemed as though people were against me and in fact, I had enemies. As I wept, prayed, and pleaded to God, I had hope and confidence that he would vindicate, answer me, and come quickly to me. Things were serendipitous in occurrence. Messages were arising precisely in a time of need. Fasting and praying until I would get a breakthrough.

> *Wait for the Lord, be strong, take heart and wait for the Lord. (Psalm 27:14)*

As I read this Psalm, a message in text came from my favorite speaker. "God has already prepared the way now he's just preparing you." "Give God your weakness, and he will give you his strength."

Rhema word was coming straight down from heaven to me. I was desperately searching for deliverance. In a moment of weakness, I picked up the phone, calling the church office crying my eyes out. I asked to speak with one of the pastors to get an unbiased perspective. After all, I was emotionally wounded therefore could not see anything beyond my pain.

Someone agreed to counsel me, explaining the incident surrounding the probation, I was instructed to allow leaders to handle any future disagreements from this point forward keeping my hands clean and free from any drama or chaos. Moving past the original incident to my aggressive reaction when confronted, I was asked "What's really going on? Mistrust? Power struggles?"

They then stated I was insecure and had power struggles. "How did you know?" I replied.

In amazement, he could see right through me, so I thought, strangely enough, as I am writing this book, it was the exact words I had written prior to our counseling. WHOAH! I couldn't believe the serendipitous alignment of my writings to his declaration. I knew God was with me, as this was not a coincidence. They relayed their personal struggles in this area which were an amazement and a comfort to me.

They explained God's design for different methods of teaching, abilities, and personalities.

After the conversation, I had a shift in thinking and a different perspective. Asking them for instructions on how to amend this relationship, they advised me to go to this person in humility and acknowledge my willingness to be under their authority and submission. I agreed to verbalize this directly and made an appointment to apologize. Swallowing my pride, doing one of the hardest things I have ever done, acknowledging my wrongs face to face. I confessed my errors in defiance and rebellion against authority, my pride, and verbally causing harm by shredding words. Despite fear and sloth, I proceeded in faith and courage, knowing this was walking in obedience to God, pursuing peace, and asking for forgiveness. I knew if I didn't make this right, I would never be right before God.

> *Now we ask you brothers to respect those who work hard among you, who are over you and admonish you. Hold them in the highest regard because of their work. Live in peace with each other. (1 Thessalonians 5:12-13)*

I submitted to God's authority to correct my mistake, leaving my offering at the altar, making peace with my brethren. 1 Thessalonians 5: 22 says If anyone is angry with his brother, he will be subject to judgment. We are instructed to leave our gift there in front of the altar then be reconciled to your brother. Knowing scripture and meditating on his word means there is no debating on what to do or when to act. Afterward, I was grateful it was over, and amends were received. I was still having a hard time recovering from this humiliation.

I refused to go back to my church due to embarrassment and pride. This created another issue since stepping back and away lead to isolation and depression. During this withdrawal, substituting worship and biblical teaching with heavy metal and trance music, I deepened my abyss. I was obscured from God's light and power, allowing darkness to penetrate my soul and flood my spirit and thoughts. This comes straight out of my journal.

"Thoughts of suicide and giving up flooded my mind and soul. Deep agony envelopes me, causing me to weep sorrowfully, literally hitting my face, asking God why he ever made me?"

Why would you ever make someone like me? I wanted to die instead of suffering this miserable existence. Knowing relapse would be the end for me, sexual sin would deepen this self-hatred and suicide would grieve my parents, orphan my animals, disappoint and devastate my friend and employer. I was afraid the women I speak to so boldly in front of might question their own professed faith? These thoughts were a flash of danger! Not wanting to risk losing the things God had so richly blessed me with nor risk the possibility of sealing my eternal fate forever. This I could not allow! Immediately I called my sponsor, desperately needing to be talked off the cliff! One of the reasons I am still sober today is I use her and am brutally honest with her and heed her instructions.

She proceeded to instruct me the key is in step seven. We asked God to remove every single defect of our character, all my defects of character that are blocking me from God's power. Every day all day, praying before the Lord that he eradicates my seven deadly sins. I had them all, pride, anger, jealousy, sloth, greed, and lust for power, envy, and gluttony. I wanted it all and was angry that I wasn't getting it.

From this incident, and previous similar incidents, I realize how fragile and insecure I was, and how much I struggled for prestige and power my entire life. It was always about not being or having enough and climbing to the top to get it and finding ways to attain rank, fame, validation, and power.

From adoption at birth, not measuring up in life, rejection, and abandonment in relationships, this deep root has manifested in every area of my life past bringing it full circle to my present. Along with this prayer, "My Creator, I am now willing that you have all of me, good and bad. I pray that you remove every single defect of my character that stands in the way of my usefulness to you and my fellows. I pray that you grant me the strength as I go from here to do your bidding. Amen.

I prayed and fasted from all types of music, no more music, no more distractions. God and I in solitude to break this stronghold, and healing began to take place. A lot of things were intertwining concerning humility and correction.

Returning to the incident concerning the client and the candy bar. When she asked my coworker to perform her service, I was indignant! This coworker corrected me on my rudeness and the need to apologize. The last thing in the world I wanted to do was take advice and corrective criticism, admitting I was wrong, especially from someone 20 years younger than me! Anyone but her to give me advice, please! I looked at her and asked how I would even begin this conversation?

I had a revelation. This inextricable situation I had caused by lack of emotional balance and spiritual maturity had to be rectified, but how? What would I say? Keep in mind, while all of this was going on at my church, I was stripped of power, position, and dignity. Brought low in spirit and attitude, I felt despised, ridiculed, humiliated, and worthlessness.

Meanwhile, I had been taking this dissatisfaction out on everyone around me. We discussed an idea on how to engage; I would call this client, again making another apology. What a hard pill to swallow, being both proud and wrong. Yielding and agreeing to this younger coworker, these humiliations, yet again were designed and intended by God to refine and mold my character. How painful to be stripped in front of everyone.

> *Whoever loves discipline loves knowledge, but he who hates correction is stupid. (Proverbs 12:1)*
>
> *A fool shows his annoyance at once but a prudent man overlooks an insult. (Proverbs 12:16)*
>
> *He who ignores discipline comes to poverty and shame but he whoever heeds correction is honored. (Proverbs 13:18)*
>
> *The fear of the Lord teaches a man wisdom and humility comes before honor. (Proverbs 15:33)*

I called the client, explaining the incident that created my despair and depression. I owned my unprofessional misconduct, as well as apologized for my selfishness, inconsideration, and unkindness. I informed her of my coworkers' inability to perform my job, as well as my inability to perform theirs. Asking this woman for forgiveness and understanding in accepting my amends, I promised this conduct would never occur again. She did, in fact, accept my apology, therefore giving me another chance.

Truthfully, what seemed so difficult and humiliating, initially turned out to be a blessing. I kept a good client, gained order back at my place of work, and was grateful I took a wallop in humility, heeding correction and advice from my coworker because she was right, I was wrong, and in the end, everyone was better by it, especially me.

If our hearts are right before God, then our relationships with others can be made right too. When our hearts have been cleansed from sin and reconciled to God you will begin to see a difference in the way we treat others. (Deuteronomy 11:1-25 NIV Chronological study notes)

> *Blessed are the poor in spirit, for theirs is the kingdom of heaven. Blessed are those who mourn, for they will be comforted. Blessed are the meek, for*

they will inherit the earth. Blessed are those who hunger and thirst for righteousness, for they will be filled. Blessed are the merciful, for they will be shown mercy. Blessed are the pure in heart, for they will see God. Blessed are the peacemakers for they will be called sons of God. (Matthew 5:3-9)

Driving truth from my head to my heart, making new patterns (grooves) in my brain, resulting in transformed behavior, and obeying God is where transformation occurs. The beatitudes can be understood as a code of ethics, a standard for believers. They contrast Kingdom values from worldly values. They should be taken as a whole and describe what followers of Christ should be like. Not that I can fully attain perfection; however, this is God's standard for us.

I began to repent of my idolatry, selfish ambition, and desire for rank, position, and prestige. Holding my position in leadership like a badge of honor, then to lose it was a devastating blow. I practiced vigilance in prayer, releasing all offenses at the feet of Jesus. I took authority over lies, rejection, and unworthiness. I repented of idolatry because my identity was wrapped up in a position rather than in

Christ, no matter how humbling, God was allowing it.

I wanted to run or bail like I always had past instead of eating the bread of adversity, but if I did, I would remain childish, proud, and sabotage my growth as well as my destiny. Continuous, constant abiding in Christ and meditating on his word rather than the world for answers, I began gaining mastery over offenses, rejection, strife, and unworthiness. Believing my position as a leader was still secure during this ninety-day probation period, I ate crow.

I continued attending class as a way of being surrendered, compliant, and agreeable. Week after week I attended and was instructed to sit in the back, not to share, and to only listen. So being submissive to their authority as I was instructed by one of the pastors who counseled me, I did what was asked of me in humility and obedience. When I raised my hand to share later as the weeks passed, I typically was overlooked. When I did participate and was called on, comments to me alone were to keep it brief and get to the point. I felt so berated, only enduring this ridicule and almost a punishment with an end in sight; completion of being restored to a leadership position. Thinking if I endured this hardship, humiliation, and opposition, learned the lesson, finished my sentence, I would regain position and be restored.

All my life, my worth has been in my accomplishments and abilities. I felt valued because of my performance, my body, my looks, and my ability to thrive competing for men and money. All these faulty sources of power, significance, and identity were being ripped from me, utterly stripped away. For the first time, I was being made nothing and was allowing it. I couldn't run, hide, or pretend anymore. I was being stripped to the core, tolerating and enduring it; after all, everything I have endured thus far in my journey was brutal and hardcore, so I had already been equipped for the suffering. This was just another level of suffering and growth. Suffering, being pruned by God to have every part of me, root and branch. Throw every weight that hinders me into the fire to be burned.

In trying to have it all Rehoboam lost almost everything. Motivated by greed and power he pressed to hard and divided his kingdom. He didn't need more money because he had already inherited the richest kingdom in the world. He didn't need more power because he was king. His demands were based on selfishness rather than spiritual discernment. Those who insist on having it all end up with little or nothing. Rehoboam's foolishness divided his kingdom. (see 2 Chronicles 10:16-19)

Coming home from class one evening, instead of reacting to these humiliations or punishments, I went straight for wisdom and comfort in God's word. There I discovered a direct Rhema word from God. Free falling right in the book of Samuel was a divine word to me. I discovered in 1 Samuel 16:7 the story of David being called last after all his brothers were selected to be viewed as the next king. People look at the outer appearance; God looks at the heart. A whisper came from God. David was overlooked but appointed king.

Speaking to my sponsor the following day, she observed that I'm not enjoying the group anymore. After her counsel, the decision to step down and maximize my service, time and potential where the most impact would be. Inquiring to this leader where my standing was now that "probation" had ended, I was told leadership had ended due to many internal issues within the group.

I have an expression, "nothing is wasted." Although the original purpose I had been attending was no longer relevant, nothing was wasted, for I would have dropped out long ago. God allowed this testing. I certainly endured things in retrospect that are now valuable.

My son if you come forward to serve the Lord prepare yourself for temptation. Set your heart right and steadfast, do not be hasty in times of calamity. Cleave to him do not depart, that you may be honored at the end of your life. Accept whatever is brought upon you, and in changes that humble you be patient. For gold is tested in the fire and acceptable men in the furnace of humiliation. Trust in him he will help you. Make your ways straight and hope in him. You who fear the Lord hope for good things, for everlasting joy and mercy. Consider the ancient generations and see whoever trusted in the Lord and was put to shame? Whoever persevered in fear of the Lord and was forsaken? Whoever called on Him and was overlooked? For the Lord is compassionate and merciful. He forgives and saves in time of affliction.

This prayer was sent to me by my sponsor at exactly the time I needed it. As the pressure and heat intensified, my roots drove deeper into the ground for living water which is Christ.

Chapter 10

Closing Doors

During this season of reckoning and correction, I was dating the same man. I was certainly experimenting. After all, this was my first real relationship ever. I wouldn't call it stable either. It was a battleground, a science project, LOL!!! When the phone call came and he told me that it just wasn't working for him anymore and he needed to let go, I was relieved. I understood. I responded with gratitude for all he had done for me and how well he had treated me.

I had been pulling away for some time after every setback. It took time to heal and reestablish the footing where we once were. Each time would destroy all the progress we had made, ultimately regressing over time. Losing all ground when restarting, rebuilding a foundation all over again, and he certainly didn't have the patience for this.

Coming from so much trauma, I couldn't run ahead to the place where we left off. He was so enamored, he was suffocating and overbearing, which made me withdraw all the more. However sad I may feel, I must put away my selfishness and let him go. I need to release him one hundred percent, instead of selfishly selecting the pieces I want, discarding the scraps, yanking him around like a yo-yo.

Letting go meant closing doors with Danny and leadership. With both things occurring in succession, there was grief, sorrow, and a great sense of loss to me. Grieving the loss of a friend, sad of actually losing him, but I decided to endure momentary emptiness and sorrow in exchange for trusting God's plan, provision, and purpose through the pain. Instead of hanging on selfishly, I fearfully let go and held faithfully, desperately to my refuge and strength, Almighty God.

Depressed refers to a lapse in buoyancy because of fatigue and unhappiness due to a sense of being unable to change unsatisfactory conditions. Yes, there is sadness, but at the same time, hope, a comfort in knowing the God of the Universe, gives time and attention to every detail concerning me.

Grief is a process, and I will arrive, only visiting for a moment. It is not a permanent destination to end engulfed in self-pity and darkness.

Do I understand the difference between dejection, selection, rejection, and incompatibility? At this time, this man and I are definitely incompatible. I have a whole lot of growing up to do, and he has his issues. Along with growing up, I need healing from brokenness past—physical, emotional, mental, and sexual abuse. I needed healing and restoration from unworthiness to wholeness and healing from past abuse and pain and walking in forgiveness and redemption.

Instead of focusing on the absence or dissatisfaction, I am choosing to focus on the opportunity this brought into my life. It was God's gift of allowing me to experience a quality of courting and endearment never known before. This man truly cared about me without a sexual exchange. A new experience of being loved for who I am, not for gratifying someone sexually, who enjoyed and valued my companionship and friendship, even with nothing more. This opportunity allowed me to walk through the process of sexual purity. Being rooted and established in my foundation with Christ, unwavering in God's standards, and adopting them as true and the standard in which I wanted to adopt as my own. For the first time, I was unmoved, fixed in an area where before, I had no boundaries or standards at all.

It was empowering and liberating to choose God, obeying him, honoring him above anyone else. Before this relationship, fear and doubt existed. I was doubtful if I would find someone who would honor me in this way. God revealed to me that I could find that person. Thank you for allowing me to work out my salvation with fear and trembling.

> *Therefore, my beloved, just as you have always obeyed, not only in my presence, but even more in my absence, continue to work out your salvation with fear and trembling. (Philippians 2:12)*

An additional motive for believers working out their sanctification is understanding the consequences of their sin. Changing my perspective, this was a gift from God when someone provided financially where in the past, I was always the meal ticket. Someone respected and honored me, where previously fear of disapproval and rejection remained. When I take God's view on the matter, this isn't a loss at all; it is a gain, a victory. Conquering lies, fear, rejection, and doubt with resurrection power and truth.

I understand I have much to learn as a human being and as a child of God, who I am, what I want, or don't. Perhaps I am not ready to form a true partnership with another human being, not at this time. Sometimes stepping back and away allows me to process emotions and deal with adolescences. Regardless of the other person's imperfections, it is my responsibility to examine my own. Stepping back means taking time to re-evaluate myself and make the necessary corrections for growth.

Selecting growth by enduring discomfort, rejecting temporary fixes, or gratifications that ultimately leave me unfulfilled and remorseful, I opted for God's healing and comfort during mourning and his perspective during this time of loss to only discover how much I had gained by this experience. This allowed me to see how much growth and progress I had made. Never before have I obeyed God's standard, denied my flesh, looked to him, and through the lens of scripture for answers, healing, comfort, deliverance, and restoration. I was taking it from the pages of the Bible and walking it out in my daily life. I gained a new perspective that every event in my life has significance if I search out the true meaning and look for the lesson.

Sad Leadership

Closing doors with an intimate relationship and on a leadership position was painful. It was frustrating because I wasted so much time, continuing to attend without a purpose. Once again, I was learning that God allows free will, everything is allowed by God for his ultimate purposes. When I chose to disobey and have fits of rage, it was ultimately a separating, a sifting, if you will, to bring what is unfit in me to the surface.

I was managing my strongholds, so I thought, now I see they were managing me. Now as I look back, I can see how painfully necessary all this was to crucify the pride of being in a position in order to realize my worth and identity of only being in a relationship with Jesus Christ. Crucifying my pride, envy, selfishness, and greed for power at the cross. All I think I deserve, my rights, and desires had to be laid at the feet of Jesus. Nailing it all to the cross. My rights become demands, demands insist on having my way or having it all, which in turn leaves me angry, crippled, and discontent with life. I constantly vacillated between God's wisdom, understanding, and forgiveness to hurt, offense, anger, wrath, and malice.

Pridefully, I think how unfair it all is, being strung along, keeping my hopes up. Unforgiving, having a hard time releasing judgment, conviction, and justice to God Almighty where justice and judgment belong. All I can do is grieve aloud to the Lord in this situation.

This was one of the most difficult offenses to overcome and release to God. I didn't know why it hurts so much, what to pray for, or how to overcome? All I could do was grieve to the Lord. My anger was keeping me fueled and burning. Most certainly, this anger was unrighteous because no anger should outlast a day. This was recurring and suffocating, I needed to be free and rid of it, but how? I could feel the dark forces closing in and choking me, the war waging within, pulling me under.

> *In the same way the spirit comes to us, helps us in our weaknesses. We do not know what to pray for, or how to offer it worthily as we ought, but the Holy Spirit himself goes to meet our supplications and pleas with unspeakable yearnings to deep for utterance. (Romans 8:26)*

> *For we do not have a high priest who is unable to empathize with our weaknesses but was tempted in*

every way just as we are yet did not sin. (Hebrews 4:15)

O people of Zion who live in Jerusalem, you will weep no more. How gracious he will be when we cry for help! Although the Lord gives you the bread of adversity and the water of affliction. The Lord teacher will instruct them and this time they will respond with obedience. This is the way walk in it. (Isaiah 30:19-21)

A contrast in attitude. As I cry and seek, all of this is coming forth page after page.

Do you not know? Have you not heard? The Lord is the everlasting God, the Creator of the ends of the earth. He will not grow tired or weary, and his understanding no one can fathom. He gives strength to the weary and increases the power of the weak. Even youths grow tired and weary, and young men stumble and fall; but those who hope in the Lord will renew their strength. They will soar on wings like eagles; they will run and not grow weary, they will walk and not be faint. (Isaiah 40:28-31)

> *"But you, Israel, my servant, Jacob, whom I have chosen, you descendants of Abraham my friend, I took you from the ends of the earth, from its farthest corners I called you. I said, 'You are my servant'; I have chosen you and have not rejected you. So do not fear, for I am with you; do not be dismayed, for I am your God. I will strengthen you and help you; I will uphold you with my righteous right hand. (Isaiah 41:8-10)*

Do not be afraid. How many times does he tell me not to be afraid? The Lord, your redeemer, the Holy One of Israel, promises to be my protector, Father, comforter and my shield.

From my own experience, no matter how much I cry or pray when something is blocking me from God's power, my prayers aren't heard, or should I say unanswered. Not that God is removed from caring or his Holy Spirit is absent, but when dealing with a Holy God the sin must be dealt with in order to have complete access. When I have trash in my heart that first needs to be acknowledged, then disposed. God isn't comfortable in a contaminated or polluted environment.

During my recovery, I have learned an inventory process that identifies the old idea or lie I am living in, and replacing it with a new idea or truth I am willing to adapt in its place. I know my seven deadly sins and shortcomings, how everything above leaves me with feelings of separation, and five negative personality traits. When I set this all on paper, it is eye-opening, powerful, and humbling especially when confessed to another human being.

How brutally honest and transparent for me to allow total strangers to peer into my heart, mind, and life. To see what only God and my sponsor sees. Laying it all on the line is to help someone struggling or immobilized with feelings of irrelevance, inferiority, indifference, isolation, not belonging, rejection, and unworthiness. For so many of us, we have these emotions, self-defeating thoughts or behaviors, and are unequipped on how to overcome or resolve them? By allowing you to experience my pain, lies of the enemy, weakness, frailty, and all my raw, good, bad, and ugly is to reveal a level of authenticity and humility.

Old Idea - Lie	Affect	Defect	Negative Traits
If I am not approved of or chosen, I'm worthless	*Self-esteem Mental and Emotional Security Rank Power Prestige Position*	*Greed - I want it all Notoriety Respect Pride Anger Envy - of others being chosen and getting away with it*	*Indignant Jealous Vengeful Unforgiving Wrathful*
New Idea - Truth	**Separation**	**Shortcomings**	**Positive Traits**
I'm enough with God, God has approved of me, He has chosen me, His approval is all I need.	*Set apart Isolated Disunited*	*Selfish Self-Seeking Frightened*	*I will strive to be Humble Faithful Mature Accepting Secure Patient*

I am broken without God, nothing without him. He is my righteousness, redemptive, resurrecting power is in him alone. In revealing so many of these flaws in my makeup that are difficult but necessary to admit, is to come alongside of you with deep compassion, empathy, and understanding. This is a necessary ongoing process of self-examination and repentance to identify the exact nature of my wrongs, admit, repent, and ask God to remove them.

When my inventory was complete, I asked my Creator to have all of me good and bad. I wanted Him to remove every single defect of character, root and branch, that stood in the way of his usefulness and effectiveness. I was praying Thy will be done along with the power and strength to carry it out. Once admission of my faults to God and my sponsor had occurred, the barrier was broken, where bondage once existed, I experienced new life, power, freedom, and peace. Hallelujah!

Chapter 11

Opening the Door For the Enemy

When Satan finished tempting Jesus, he left him until the next opportunity came (see Luke 4:13). And so it goes, the next opportunity came for me also.

> *Be sober, vigilant, because your adversary the devil walketh about seeking whom he may devour. (1 Peter 5:8)*

I was walking in authority over lies, attacks, and schemes of the enemy. Any attempts or whispering lies that came to mind, I quickly cast down. I rejected the lies and imaginations from the evil forces. Knowing there's a liar, deceiver, a roaring lion seeking to devour me, destroy my peace, my future, and ultimately kill me, I was fighting a battle in the invisible realm. I was taking the helmet of salvation, guarding my mind and thoughts against the adversary.

Take the helmet of salvation and the sword of the spirit which is the word of God. (Ephesians 6:17)

Nothing was defeating me. I knew to entertain these whispers was a death trap. Entertaining any idea contrary to God's truth was taking poison and giving the enemy ample ammunition. Like Eve in the garden, she entertained the serpent's lies and disregarded God's commands. After all, I knew better than to be deceived and doubt God's commands.

In Genesis 3:3, God warned Eve that she must not eat or touch it if you do, you will die. I knew better than to touch it or eat it, for surely, I would die. Not in a literal sense, but a spiritual sense. The abyss I just climbed out of was worse than death. It was agonizing, unbearable, mental and emotional, separation, darkness, and misery. I thought to myself, this is it! Alas, I have the secrets to walking triumphantly above the circumstances!

I have more understanding now reflecting on this incident. How quickly my words and allowing the negative words of others to penetrate my mind and spirit.

> *Likewise the tongue is a small part of the body but it makes great boasts. Consider what a great forest fire is set on fire by a small spark. The tongue also is a fire, a world of evil among the parts of the body. It corrupts the whole person, sets the whole course of his life on fire, and is itself set on fire by hell. (James 3:5-6)*

I ran into a fellow church member who wasn't attending any longer, and when I asked how they were and where they had been, boy did they tell me all about it. They, like me, had been offended and left disgruntled. When I allowed their negative spew onto me without interrupting them, and immediately taking it to prayer for healing, restoration, forgiveness, and peace, it opened my wound that was in the process of being healed. By allowing this negativity to invade my personal space, demonic influences were activated. By engaging in this conversation with her and opening my mouth speaking curses, all progress and healing that was taking place were negated.

Looking back, I see the devil's craftiness, plotting, patiently waiting for another opportunity; I, on the other hand, was unprepared, leaving me unexpectedly falling into a different booby trap.

Being double-minded, thinking two different ways, I received nothing from the Lord. (James 1:6-8)

Something I have since learned as with Eve in the garden, the enemy wants me to keep my eyes off God's goodness, focusing on what I don't have or didn't get, suggesting God is withholding from me. Conversations have come to me since and instead of looking at other's advancements, or accomplishments as a negative, looking at myself in comparison, I know to believe God has my absolute best in mind, being secure in his provision, adoration, and unwavering love for me. Being authentically happy for the success of others, while believing, not doubting in the precision, timing, and destiny of mine. This new attitude and awareness came of course, after many crushing blows. There is still more suffering and hard work to be done.

After realizing what I had done and undone, I quickly set a boundary with this individual never to speak of this incident again. Together we prayed over the phone a prayer of repentance of slander, gossip, and unforgiveness, binding in prayer any attacks of the enemy, binding abandonment, disapproval, rejection, bitterness, unworthiness, and unforgiveness and losing forgiveness, healing, restoration, and God's all-encompassing love.

> *Truly I tell you, whatever you bind on earth will be bound in heaven, and whatever you loose on earth will be loosed in heaven. (Matthew 18:18)*

Paramount things to remember and practice:
- Keeping my eyes on Christ
- Keeping my focus in front of me and in my own lane
- Praise and gratitude for all his wonderful works
- Believing and trusting in God's goodness and faithfulness past being the same forward
- Keeping my thoughts excellent, praiseworthy and true
- Keeping my speech excellent, praiseworthy and true
- Repentance being a lifestyle-keeping an open channel with God

When I put these things into practice, I am in less danger of falling into the enemy's plan.

Chapter 12

Waiting on God

As I moved forward in times of solitude, fasting, and prayer, the Lord came to me, speaking to me through the scriptures. David was overlooked by men yet chosen by God to be king. David was anointed to be king at age sixteen. He didn't become king until he was thirty—fourteen years of waiting.

Not knowing this when reading it, I found comfort, understanding, and assurance in God's process, timing, and order when I don't see anything in motion. A mighty God is working behind the scenes. Fear the Lord, recognize he is all-knowing, all-powerful and all-wise. When we view God correctly, we get a better view of ourselves—weak, frail, sinful, and needy.

> *The Lord confides in those who fear him; he makes his covenant known to them. (Psalm 25:14)*

The Lord is a friend to those who fear him. God offers intimate and lasting friendship to those who revere him, who hold him in the highest honor.

> *Turn to me and be gracious to me, for I am lonely and afflicted. (Psalm 25:16)*

Do problems go from bad to worse? God is the only one who can take our problems and turn them into glorious victories.

For this fear, loneliness, and sadness, God is our only antidote (see Psalm 27). I meditated on God's word constantly; it was the only thing that gave me revelation, awakening, direction, and light in any shadows or doubt. After all, I was waiting on God and seeking answers.

I remember my affliction and my wandering, the bitterness and the gall. I well remember them, and my soul is downcast within me. Yet this I call to mind and therefore I have hope: Because of the Lord's great love we are not consumed, for his compassions never fail. They are new every morning;

great is your faithfulness. I say to myself, "The Lord is my portion; therefore I will wait for him" (Lamentations 3:19-24). In these times of affliction and suffering the more I searched for answers and comfort in the scriptures, the more enlightened of my errors I became. No matter the wrongs of others, if I continuously focus on them, I will remain disillusioned, a victim and continue to suffer injustice.

Was I treated unfairly? Was information excluded from the original incident, therefore withholding information is, in fact, omission and dishonest? Regardless, these aren't my iniquities nor my issues. The longer I focus on the injustice, I remain a victim, powerless, festering, harboring grudges and spiritually sequestered. I was slowly awakened to my errors instead of being a hall monitor, lawgiver, and judge. There is only one lawgiver and one judge, Lisa, and you're not it. By doing so, I was standing in judgment of the law.

> *For the same way you judge, you will be judged. Why do you look at the speck in your brother's eye and pay no attention to the plank in your own. (Matthew 7:3)*

Jesus tells us to examine our motives and conduct instead of judging others. This hypocritical, judgmental attitude toward others is used to tear others down to build myself up. It is not to overlook wrong behavior, but a call to be discerning rather than negative.

I need to trust God to be the final judge and leave it there (see 1 Corinthians 5:12).

Because judgment without mercy will be shown to anyone who has not been merciful. Mercy triumphs over judgment. (James 2:13)

Do I want God's judgment and wrath or his mercy, grace, and forgiveness? Constantly being reminded, I am a sinner in need of a savior, how much mercy, grace, and forgiveness I need consistently. How frequently wrong, wrong, wrong I really am. This keeps my perspective about God correct, and my desperate need of him.

The Lord is good to those whose hope is in him, to the one who seeks him; it is good to wait quietly for the salvation of the Lord. (Lamentations 3:25-26)

Salvation being deliverance, saving, help, and reclamation. Reclamation is the process of claiming something back. No matter what the price or duration of the calamity. As I look for comfort and answers in God's word, I sense an overwhelming, constant presence and assurance that he will deliver me, and I will reclaim what I lost.

Perhaps not literally or tangibly, but in a mental, emotional, and spiritual sense, reclaiming internal peace, freedom, and restored reputation and honor. In a spiritual sense, I am taking the time to learn God's ways, casting aside all pride, selfishness, and misunderstandings. When I get another perspective detached from my emotions, through the lens of truth, this penetrates the heart beyond knowledge to gaining wisdom and understanding.

> *It is good for a man to bear the yoke while he is young. The man who has seen affliction. Patiently suffering the mockery of his enemies. Let him sit alone in silence the Lord has laid it on him. (Lamentations 3:27-28)*

I know the Lord had laid it on me; therefore, I will wait. Believe me, the suffering, waiting is brutal and humiliating, but where I've already traveled through has qualified me for the test. Only now, I am beginning to grasp the depth and meaning suffering can bring to life. It can bring a dynamic quality to the

Christian's life. Like a tree driving its roots deeper to find water, instead of caving or quitting, my roots went even deeper to find water, "living water," which is Christ. As I said before, I will sit in silence and endure the suffering, for he has laid it on me.

> *For no one is cast off by the Lord forever. Though he brings grief, he will show compassion, so great is his unfailing love. (Lamentations 3:31-32)*

For men are not cast off from the Lord forever. Though he brings grief, he will show compassion, so great is his unfailing love. The same God who judges restores. Great is his faithfulness; both are used to sum up God's covenant mercies towards his people.

God's Covenant is His Contract.

> *To deprive them of justice—would not the Lord see such things? Who can speak and have it happen if the Lord has not decreed it? Is it not from the mouth of the Most High that both calamities and good things come? Why should a man complain when punished for their sins? Let us examine our ways and test them, and let us return to the Lord. (Lamentations 3:36-40)*

In Psalm 119:17, David said, "It was good that I was afflicted so I may learn your ways." Paul added, "We experience dying so that Christ can be formed within us. Until we die of self-sufficiency and are broken by God we cannot be remade by him" (2 Corinthians 4:11).

Waiting to Acceptance

One Sunday morning after worship, I wasn't in a good space. Initially I was going to speak to the associate pastor, as I had previously, but he was absent, leaving me to ask the senior pastor. When I began to utter words, only weeping and sobbing released in front of him without being able to gain control. When I spoke, all I could say is I was thinking about leaving the church. Left with a feeling of not belonging, feeling discarded like garbage, I explained that I didn't know where to go from here or what to do?

He replied, "That is straight from the pit of hell."

He added that quite the opposite was true and prompted me to set an appointment for counseling. Amazed, really? You actually want to talk to me? You are going to carve out time in your schedule for me?

Wow! That impacted my core. I was shocked as well as extremely grateful.

Waiting on God is not easy. Often it seems he is not answering our prayers or sees the urgency of our situation. This kind of thinking implies that God is unfair or not in control. To the contrary, God is in control and is worth the wait. Remember, God's silence is not indifference. God is frequently silent during a test. He calls us to hope and wait because often, God uses times of waiting to refresh, renew, and teach us. Make good use of your waiting by discovering what God may be trying to teach you.

As the day for my counseling session approached, I became more anxious, wavering in doubt. I was thinking defensively about how to present my case. Now that a dam broke in front of someone, there's no reigning back the emotional flood that took place. So now what? Whoops! There it is! Initially, my mind was operating like an attorney representing a case before a court of law or a judge. How do I present my case or represent myself? Do I come in with tons of evidence or raging with a critical spirit? Do I dredge up my perceptions of inequality or favoritism?

What prompted the explosion resulting in removal was feelings of mistrust, suspicion, and irrelevance. As the day approached, I asked for intercessory prayer knowing the power of being in agreement and joining in faith with other believers. I asked God for wisdom on how to handle this matter, revelation, and honesty to search myself while gaining truth and understanding.

Of course, knowing all these things I had joined in agreement with, what I was asking for was being unveiled and delivered to me. Profoundly, something came over me on the way home. Abiding constantly in God's presence with prayer and supplication, his still small voice overcame me. "You know Lisa, at some point you're going to have to let this go. At some point, you are going to have to come to a place of neutrality and acceptance."

God began to reveal many things to me over the days approaching my counseling session. My deadly words and outbursts deeply hurt someone, and though forgiven, perhaps not forgotten nor erased. No matter how strong we think we are in the Lord, we are still human, sensitive with emotions. Like me having a difficult time letting go and moving on, perhaps others were also.

Whatever the reason, I cannot continue speculating or assuming, staying in a self-imposed prison. Indeed, I am in mental, emotional, and spiritual bondage, cut off from accessing God's power. Creating my own misery by unforgiveness and believing a lie about my identity, purpose, worth, and significance and being wrapped up in a position instead of my identity of being in Christ. Being chosen by someone versus being chosen by God and living from his approval and validation.

When I began to surrender these strongholds and offenses at the cross—boom! A particular teaching would be right in front of me in the Bible or on a broadcast. Revelation and understanding that I need to be rich in mercy releasing my offenses to Christ in prayer. Releasing people to Jesus for conviction and judgment is God's alone, not mine. I need to remove the plank from my own eye so I can see the speck in yours, concentrating on my own brokenness and wickedness. The more I focus on your sin, I somehow feel superior, justifying myself, my sin, keeping me vexed in self-righteousness, anger, unrepentance, and unforgiveness. It leads to complete chaos, turmoil, confusion, falling right into the schemes of the enemy, right into the pit.

Am I more interested in seeking God's judgment and wrath or his mercy, grace, and forgiveness toward others? Which do I want to be administered to me? Do I love others as God commands or am

I stubbornly clinging to my rights and demanding my own way? Demanding my way keeps me striving, stubborn, and angry. Surrendering brings me low, humble before God, submissive, dependent, and trusting.

> *For the word of God is living and active, sharper than any double-edged sword it pierces even dividing soul, spirit, joints and marrow. It judges thoughts, attitudes of the heart. (Hebrews 4:12)*

He rushes in like a flood, there's no denying his word, it convicts me. Cutting right through my heart, my wicked heart, sinful, needy, and frail, falling at the feet of Jesus. Reverently bowed at his feet, he sees right through me, yet despite my flaws and brokenness, he looks at me in love, indescribable love, and outstretched arms receiving me with mercy, redemption, and grace.

He isn't standing there with a lightning bolt to strike me dead. On the contrary, when I bow reverently to him in awe and adoration of this Holy God who takes time for me, seeing all there is to see; good, bad and at times unlovable. When I am ready to trade in all I am for all he has, he is there with open arms, ready to receive me saying, come as you are, come to me. I fall. I weep because of his unfailing love that I don't deserve and cannot earn, yet there I am accepted, received, forgiven, and restored.

By the time I met with the pastor for counseling, I was in a place of neutrality. Once again, I had been delivered from bondage and was walking in victory above my circumstances. I explained the origin of the incident, the wrongs I had committed in getting involved by the coercion of another, and betraying confidence. I described the incident of conflict, correction, and probation, laying my entire heart transparent during this session. I shared my feelings of punishment, being overlooked, and cast aside. Also, the entire time, I was being edified by God in scripture with the story of David in 1 Samuel being overlooked yet God chose him. Rhema word about others overlooking David, yet he was anointed king.

Going into great detail of my writings, that every single thing I had just written was correlating through his sermons, on-air or online, affirming me by divine assurance. I knew God was leading, directing me to write my story, and I was acting in obedience. Transparently, I explained my adoption, my background, addiction, and involvement in the sex industry; and using it as a platform to minister to women in institutions. Hearing so much wisdom from this man and I was ever grateful to be understood and received with love. This all shows me the amazing results we can have when we wage war with spiritual armor, being open to God's correction as well as being open to another person's wisdom and counsel.

God again was working things out on my behalf behind the scenes as well as instructing, refining, and grooming me. I was glad I had done my work involving this coming through it and to the other side. This experience has only edified me. Edify is to instruct, improve moral character or religious knowledge. To uplift, inform, building up the soul, construction, building. Being on the other side of this meant understanding more of myself and what needs to be pruned, and allowing the Lord to do, withholding nothing.

How do we stay true to the Lord? The way to stay true to the Lord is to keep our eyes on Christ. Remembering this world is not our home, and our focus is Christ will bring everything under his control. Staying true is steadfastly resisting negative influences of false teaching and persecution. It requires perseverance when challenged or opposed. Is it possible to believe in Christ, work hard for his kingdom, and yet have broken relationships with others who are committed to the same cause?

There is no excuse for remaining not reconciled. Do not resort to cruel power plays nor stand idle, waiting for the matter to resolve itself. Instead, seek the help of those known for peacemaking. Without even realizing it, this was what I had done—being submissive to those in authority, subject to the elders.

- Daily surrender my rights to God
- Being rich in mercy toward others
- Being submissive to elders and those in authority
- Praying expectantly when aligned with God's will
- Pursue peace and reconciliation
- Admit my errors asking for forgiveness
- Pray for wisdom and it is given generously
- Pray for revelation and things will be revealed
- Release others to God in prayer
- Surrendering offenses at the cross
- Look behind the anger to the pain
- Take my pain to pain to Jesus
- Leave wrath and judgment to God for it is his alone

Chapter 13

Growing Up: Mature Faith

Putting down the substances and faulty relationships was only scratching the surface. What sank the Titanic was not the visible tip of the iceberg, but what was underneath the surface. I have maintained a manner of self-appraisal and self-discipline as a lifestyle, uncovering painful trauma, foibles, and human failings, discovering the true nature of the problem, and discarding the results. Anything blocking me from accessing his power or unfit for his kingdom purposes is discarded and thrown away. Quite frankly, this is ongoing since the propensity to sin is born within me, born into sin. Born into a broken, fallen world. The heart of man is deceitful above all things and beyond cure—who can understand it? (see Jeremiah 17:19)

For a long time, I had no self-worth, esteem, value, or identity. I said yes when I meant no, wanting so much for people to accept and approve of me. Doing anything to fit in, selling my soul for it, giving myself away in the hope of being recognized, validated, and loved. With this thwarting behavior and self-centered fear, I permitted all sorts of mistreatment, allowing others uninvited will to be imposed upon me without ever resisting or refusing. Initially, I was a victim, then afterward enraged, hitting a boiling point. I either exploded on you or imploded inwardly, finding ways to manage by sex, drugs, alcohol, money, vanity, or co-dependent relationships.

Because this was entrenched behavior, people-pleasing, approval-seeking, low self-esteem, and self-centered fear, it was difficult to solve. For some time in early recovery, it was a struggle to find my voice and establish healthy boundaries. I had to relearn the word "no" and how to communicate appropriately. Then tipping to the other extreme, I thought I should verbalize or vocalize anything annoying, inconsiderate, or disrespectful. And so, I did. To summarize the outcome, I made a lot of apologies and cleaned up several messes!

One day working on a client in my facial room, the volume of my coworkers was particularly loud.

This is always a bit of a problem, but this incident tended to be more problematic than usual. I had to come out and politely ask for everyone to please be quiet as I am in the process of performing a facial.

Returning to work in the morning with headphones on as I walked to work, I was oblivious to any noise around me. I was completely unaware of loud country music that was being played. When I did take them off, I immediately put them back on for sanity and focus. Dealing with this ongoing, obnoxious interruptions, yelling across the salon, monopolizing conversations, I proceeded to tell them about it.

Choosing to text was my first mistake as I explained the interference and lack of professionalism, explaining as adults, we should be able to communicate appropriately. Well, as you can imagine, that didn't go over well. I received denial and defiance, and oops, there it was! There were exploding words and accusations; it was messy!

Of course, I dragged my employer into this like a referee. Instead of entrusting her to manage, seeking God's wisdom and direction in prayer first, I had a sense of urgency unable to wait patiently during the process. In the past, everything I sought after was instantaneous. I've since learned God is always perfect and on time.

Fools have short fuses and explode quickly the prudent quietly shrug off insults. (Proverbs 12:16)

I was annoyed that this had been going on and felt as though nothing was being done about it. I was looking to resolve this by taking matters into my own hands. The following morning when I returned to work, a list of rules was posted in the employee kitchen.

- leave the drama at the door
- courtesy-kindness
- client professionalism
- harmony-unity between each other
- no gossip or slander of each other
- no gossip or slander of clientele
- self-examination-confession-correction of any inappropriate conduct
- fix ourselves and move on
- no level of empowerment between us

God convicted me as I read these rules. As much as I wanted to cast blame, while getting approval from my employer (salon owner), something profound came over me. A revelation from God, "I am not dealing with them at the moment I am dealing with you."

Instead of focusing on all their flaws, which were magnified tenfold in comparison to mine because of course, I'm so good. God pierced me with conviction. Do you have any of these errors in you? Do you interrupt? Do you chime in on others' conversations? Yes, I do. Are you dark and negative about coworkers in front of other clients at times? Yes, I am, and after this episode, I certainly was yesterday right in front of a client. How nonprofessional was that!!

When privately, I asked the salon owner what applies to me; she kindly pointed out "drama." Especially drama concerning Danny. Oh, how I can minimize the conduct in myself while magnifying the misconduct in others. I was painfully awakened of my desperation to get her to side with or agree with me. I was looking for approval and validation like a child while exploiting someone else.

Instead of throwing anyone under the bus, I allowed myself to soak in everything that negatively and directly applied to me—putting out of my mind the wrongs others had done, concentrating only on mine. I was deeply convicted of my wrongs and allowed truth and correction to penetrate my inner being without a deflection or distraction. This was my behavior to correct, only mine. In the quiet of my facial room, God spoke, alerting me to the fact that "You don't need to run to someone with explanations or over-explaining. Stop Lisa, stop!"

And I took every bit of discipline without fighting, rationalizing, defending minimizing or casting blame.

Did Jesus defend himself on the cross? Did he retaliate or exalt himself when mocked, despised, or rejected? No. If only I could exemplify more of my savior. I repented right on the spot to God and the owner. I asked for forgiveness of gossip, slander, rude, selfish interruptions or inappropriate conduct. Please, God, help me to be a woman of inner beauty.

> *She speaks with wisdom and faithful instructions on her unguent. Many women are noble but you surpass them all. Charm is deceptive and beauty is fleeting but a woman who fears the Lord is to be praised. Give her the reward she has earned and let her works be praised. (Proverbs 31:26, 29-30)*

God doesn't want excuses for my sin. Forgiveness requires repentance, no excuses, looking inward, point the finger at myself, taking full responsibility. All wrong conduct is rooted in sin, pride, and selfishness. Taking matters in my own hands is impatience and mistrusting God's justice and timing. He always has and will work out things for my benefit. He has my best in mind, his timing is perfect, and I can trust him.

> *The mocker seeks wisdom and finds none, but knowledge comes easily to the discerning. Stay away from a fool, for you will not find knowledge on their lips. The wisdom of the prudent is to give thought to their ways, but the folly of fools is deception. Fools mock at making amends for sin, but goodwill is found among the upright. Each heart knows its own bitterness, and no one else can share its joy. The house of the wicked will be destroyed, but the tent of the upright will flourish. (Proverbs 14:6-11)*

The prudent understand where they are going, but fools deceive themselves. Fools make fun of guilt, but the godly acknowledge it and seek reconciliation. The house of the wicked will be destroyed but the tent of the godly will flourishes. We all know mockers, people who scoff at every word of advice. They never find wisdom because they don't seek it seriously. Wisdom comes to those who apply God's word to their lives and seek out godly counselors—praying without ceasing for myself to be compassionate, understanding, and merciful while keeping my mouth closed and my prayers ascending to the throne of God for her to have revelation, humility, and peace.

When I began to pause and breath instead of allowing myself to become frustrated or annoyed, reverting to prayer, inviting God's presence to invade my personal space, my heart, and the atmosphere; only then was I relieved from irritation and annoyance. Who am I to think my way is the only way of doing things? This prejudice and perfectionism I must be rid of, but how? God, please save me from myself!!

> *So I find this law at work: Although I want to do good, evil is right there with me. For in my inner being I delight in God's law; but I see another law at work in me, waging war against the law of my mind and making me a prisoner of the law of sin at work within me. What a wretched man I am! Who will rescue me from this body that is subject to death? Thanks be to God, who delivers me through Jesus Christ our Lord! (Romans 7:21-25)*

This waging war against the law of my mind, at times I feel this literal pull, war waging against me constantly. There are times it becomes relentless and exhausting. There is great tension in our daily Christian experience. The conflict exists even though we agree with God's commands; we cannot do them. As a result, we are painfully aware of our sin.

I began to say this prayer of tolerance. God help me to believe this person is doing their absolute level best at this moment in time. Please save me from being angry, judgmental, and critical. Thy will be done.

I lifted my hands to heaven and my prayers ascending to God's throne, please save me! In the privacy of my workroom or backroom, while my hands were lifted to God on high, I began to invite his presence in the atmosphere because I needed him. I needed his grace, mercy, his presence, his love, his power, and his peace. Why? Because I certainly didn't have it on my own. Nothing good dwells in me without God. The enemy's strategy is to create division as well as dissension.

As long as I allow this chaos to manifest within, thinking I can manage or control it, I become proud, self-sufficient, doomed for failure. The moment I release my helplessness, powerlessness, and wretchedness to Jesus in complete need and desperation for him, is the moment he hears, intercedes, and grants access to his power. When I am in the presence of a

Holy God, all self-righteousness melts away. I began to look through the lens of love.

God spoke to me. I want you to be understanding, showing me another side of her upbringing and inner struggles. Instead of being indignant and condemning, I was shown compassion. I specifically asked for God's peace to cover us, as this transformed the atmosphere from chaotic to calm. Every day I prayed for peace to rain on us and for the Holy Spirit to have his way in each one of us.

Instead of fighting the forces of evil alone, I joined forces with God, asking for a heart of flesh and a sea of grace to change our hearts and atmosphere. With amazement, I watched the power of God at work. I have experienced his miraculous power in my own life but have to admit I wasn't so sure about it working in others so rapidly. When taking matters in my own hands, pointing out every area of inappropriateness or non-professionalism, it keeps me proud, self-righteous, and in inner conflict. This was new for me, not always do I need to speak out. Yes, there is a time for that, but there is a process first. A process of prayer and seeking God's guidance and wisdom allows me to get a biblical perspective instead of an emotional, carnal, and foolish one.

Allowing those in authority to resolve disputes and manage their business, and for me to mind my own. Also, I was awakened to the conviction and power of the Holy Spirit in the lives of others when we as believers ask, seek, wait, and rely on him to act. Within days, the person came into my room and apologized, saying they never apologize to anyone in their life and that I was the first. I was blown away! In return, I also apologized for my conduct.

This entire episode ended up with us hugging and being reconciled. Another reminder when we pursue righteousness and peace, relationships are ever changed. Now when annoyed at work, I immediately pray the prayer of tolerance. God, please help me believe this person is doing their absolute best. Please save me from being angry, judgmental, and critical. Thy will, not mine, be done, Amen. Save me from myself because, without a savior, I am doomed, dead in my sin.

Summing up Mature Faith, it is easy to be kind to others when things are going well, but can we still be kind when others are treating us unfairly? God wants to make us mature and complete not to keep us from all pain. Mature and complete indicates spiritual wholeness. It is not attaining perfection, nevertheless whole.

> *Consider it pure joy, my brothers and sisters, whenever you face trials of many kinds, because you know that the testing of your faith produces perseverance. Let perseverance finish its work so that you may be mature and complete, not lacking anything. (James 1:2-4)*

I need to remember God's primary concern is not to keep me from all pain, but by enduring pain, it is to make us whole, complete and lacking nothing.

Summary: Pivotal Things to Ponder

- I need to acknowledge my lack of power.
- Admit I have a problem and need help.
- I spend time with what I love; how much time am I spending with God?
- Am I investing the same amount of energy and effort into my recovery as I did my addiction?
- Am I giving God my all or only my leftovers?
- My best thinking got me here. I need a godly sponsor or mentor.
- This mentor must be trustworthy with victory in the area of addiction or overcoming strongholds.
- I need to engage and be involved.
- Participation and accountability are vital to success.

- The more I invest, the more I have to lose. The deeper and greater these investments and relationships are, the greater sense of obligation and loss if fail.

- Am I willing to take advice, accept correction, trusting they have my best in mind and speaking from their own experiences?

- Honesty with my sponsor is a deep, rich investment in this relationship.

- Cutting all ties from the past—sexual, relational, and environmental.

- Legitimate employment-making an honest living.

- Reading, meditating, memorizing scripture to understand what God has to say about a matter. Remember, my best thinking got me here.

- There was a long process of legal, financial, physical and relational consequences. I need to persist with determination, faith, and courage to rebuild the demolition I have made.

- This mess I have made wasn't overnight, therefore being patient with this process.

- When I trust in God with my whole heart, acknowledge him in all my ways, he makes way for me. There are no quick fixes or instantaneous results. Let patience have its perfect work.

- Daily we must choose to center our life around God.
- Join with others for intercessory prayer.
- Put your money where it matters. Tithing, giving of yourself, time, and resources.
- Being disciplined daily with a schedule and routine. Plan your day around God. He wants to be first, not last.
- Stay in the middle of the herd; the weak and vulnerable get picked off.
- What I think is how I feel, how I feel is how I act. Keeping my thoughts excellent, praiseworthy, and true.
- There's always something to be grateful about, find it!
- Keep a clear channel with God. If I make a mistake, own it, confess it and fix it.
- Keep short accounts with God as well as others. Ask for forgiveness from God and others.
- Keeping my side of the street clean is my responsibility. If I have 2% of the problem, it is my 2% to fix.

- Keep my eyes fixed on Christ and in my lane. This saves me a lot of grief, envy, and apologies.

- Pain is an indicator that brokenness exists. When I am disturbed, I am wrong no matter what the cause.

- Look behind the anger for your pain. Leave my pain at the cross.

- Self-examination with a written moral inventory is vital. When I write out the old idea. replacing it with a new one, the effects, defects, and shortcomings, then I can then get specific, asking God to remove them.

- When I clearly see my part, admission of flaws, it smacks me right between the eyes with no denial or casting blame.

- Getting into the depths of my soul, my worth, identity, and value as a child of God and nothing more.

- God alone is my source, provider, my healer, my comfort, my justice, defender, and my peace.

- When I find God is all I have; I will also find he is all I need.

- Rejecting lies and imaginations with trust and truth in God's goodness, great love for me, and his plans for me.
- I am unique and one of a kind. Therefore, comparison is impossible.
- When struggling with personalities with others, keep my mouth closed, and my prayers lifted to the throne of God.
- Inviting him into every situation and asking him to flood the atmosphere with his presence and peace.
- Have I ceased fighting anyone or anything?
- Daily surrendered my rights and demands to God?
- The earth is the Lord's and everything in it. God owns everyone and everything.
- There is one lawgiver and one judge, God himself.

www.ingramcontent.com/pod-product-compliance
Lightning Source LLC
Chambersburg PA
CBHW070804100426
42742CB00012B/2242